Slaves of Fear:
A Land Unconquered

An Artorian Novel

D1602586

James Mace

Legionary Books
Meridian, Idaho 83642, USA
http://www.legionarybooks.net

First eBook Edition: 2016

Published in the United States of America
Legionary Books

You wish to rule over the world, yet what surprise that many will not accept your slavery?

\- Caratacus

The Works of James Mace

Note: In each series or combination of series', all works are listed in chronological sequence

The Artorian Chronicles
Soldier of Rome: The Legionary
Soldier of Rome: The Sacrovir Revolt
Soldier of Rome: Heir to Rebellion
Soldier of Rome: The Centurion
*Empire Betrayed: The Fall of Sejanus
Soldier of Rome: Journey to Judea
Soldier of Rome: The Last Campaign
*Centurion Valens and the Empress of Death
*Slaves of Fear: A Land Unconquered

The Great Jewish Revolt and Year of the Four Emperors
Soldier of Rome: Rebellion in Judea
Soldier of Rome: Vespasian's Fury
Soldier of Rome: Reign of the Tyrants
Soldier of Rome: Rise of the Flavians

Napoleonic Era
Forlorn Hope: The Storming of Badajoz
I Stood With Wellington
Courage, Marshal Ney

* Stand-alone novel or novella with a direct tie-in to a given series

Table of Contents

Preface
Chapter I: Valeria's Elite
Chapter II: Shadows from the Past
Chapter III: Brothers' Reunion and an Emperor's Lament
Chapter IV: Delivered by Neptune
Chapter V: Slaves of Fear
Chapter VI: Finding the Enemy
Chapter VII: A Sacrifice of Blood
Chapter VIII: Chasing Ghosts
Chapter IX: Field of Sorrow
Chapter X: To the Sea
Chapter XI: Heading North, Heading Home
Chapter XII: Consort to the Empire
Chapter XIII: Winter's Cold Embrace
Chapter XIV: Valley of Riches
Chapter XV: To Tame a Land
Chapter XVI: Here We Will Stand
Chapter XVII: Hard as Iron
Chapter XVIII: A Triumph of Steel
Chapter XIX: Freedom or Slavery
Chapter XX: Heart of the Empire
Historical Afterward

Preface

Four years have passed since the Roman invasion of Britannia. Though the imperial legions won a number of spectacular victories during the initial conquest, the imperial governor, Ostorius Scapula, realizes that Emperor Claudius declared victory far too soon. An ever-volatile land, hostile forces exist even amongst loyalists and allies. To the north the allied kingdom of the Brigantes is on the verge of civil war, while to the west Rome's old nemesis, Caratacus, has returned. A former prince of the conquered Catuvellauni, he seeks revenge for the death of his brother and the subjugation of their people.

For Centurion Magnus Flavianus, the years have been beset by nightmares and sleepless nights, brought on by the slaying of his lover and their unborn child. Despite his age and the numerous scars that mar both his body and spirit, he stalwartly remains with his legion as it prepares to face Caratacus. Across the mountainous reaches of western Britannia, in the land now known as Wales, Magnus hopes to find both atonement and peace within his tormented soul.

Cast of Characters

Romans

Magnus Flavianus – A centurion primus ordo with Legio XX, Valeria

Gaius Caelius Gurges – Magnus' optio

Lucius Tyranus Costa – Centurion Primus Pilus of Legio XX, and Magnus' superior officer

Marcus Furius Corda – A recently promoted centurion primus ordo

Metellus Artorius Posthumous – Commander of the legion's Fifth Cohort

Publius Ostorius Scapula – Governor of Britannia

Gaius Suetonius Paulinus – Commanding Legate of Legio XX, newly arrived in Britannia

Julianus Flavus – Commander of Indus' Horse Regiment of Cavalry

Britons

Caratacus – Prince of the Catuvellauni and leader of the Britannic resistance to the Roman occupation

Amminus – Caratacus' youngest brother, and a staunch Roman loyalist

Eurgain – Caratacus' wife

Jago – Caratacus' son, who is soon coming of age

Sorcha – Caratacus' young daughter

Orin – King of the Silures

Seisyll – King of the Ordovices

Cartimandua – Queen of the Brigantes, allies of Rome

Venutius – Cartimandua's estranged consort, who is conspiring with Caratacus against Rome

Elisedd – Chief of the Deceangli, a tribe along the northern coast of Wales, under the protection of King Seisyll

Tathal – High druid and religious mentor to both Silures and Ordovices

Alaric – A member of Cartimandua's court

Landon – Friend of Alaric, who volunteers as an interpreter for the Romans

Chapter I: Valeria's Elite

Camulodunum, Eastern Britannia
April, 48 A.D.

Legionaries conducting javelin practice

Though the day was overcast, it was unusually warm for the early Britannic springtime. The rhythmic cadence of hundreds of feet marching along the open field were accented by the chirping of birds and the calls of other indigenous beasts. The tall grasses were still damp from the night-time rains, which soaked the feet and ankles of the advancing force of imperial Roman legionaries. They soon came to a halt, the occasional glimpse of the sun reflecting off their metal armour and brightly painted shields.

"*Cohort!*" the centurion primus pilus shouted.

"*Century!*" his subordinate centurions primus ordo called over their shoulders.

"*Advance!*"

Eight hundred pairs of sandaled feet immediately stepped off, keeping behind their shields, their synched footfalls beating a dull tempo into the earth. They were in loose battle formation with each soldier covering a frontage of six feet.

These men were not simply legionaries; they were the elite First Cohort of Legio XX, Valeria. Better trained than their comrades in the regular cohorts, they were hand-picked veterans, each of whom had earned his place, usually after at least sixteen years of service in the ranks. On rare occasions, a soldier would be elevated at a slightly younger age, while many who had the required time-in-service were denied entry into the cohort. Significantly older than the majority of their mates, they varied in age from early thirties to mid-forties, yet the years of conditioning and training allowed them to move with the speed and precision of much younger men.

The First Cohort had only five centuries, instead of the usual six. However, each of these was at double strength of one hundred and sixty legionaries as opposed to eighty. They were also the only cohort that was always kept at full strength. Whenever one of its soldiers retired from the ranks or passed on to the gods, the commanding centurions of the cohort would scour the rolls of the legion to find replacements. And unlike the rest of the legion, those elevated into the First Cohort were exempt from any sort of fatigue detail. They were also better paid. Their legionaries made almost the same wage as a decanus leading an eight-man squad in the regular cohorts. And because they were exempt from menial labour, these elite troops spent most of the duty day training to do what they knew best, what all soldiers of Rome were first and foremost expected to excel at.

"First, Second, and Third Centuries…wedge formation!"

With speed and precision, the double-strength centuries rapidly compressed their files and each formed into a massed wedge. The commanding centurion of each element stood at its apex. His optio positioned himself at the very back, ensuring formation integrity. The remaining two centuries stayed in their standard battle formation of six ranks, as they advanced on the flanks of the wedges. From above, the formation would have resembled the teeth of a beast or perhaps the wide tips of an enormous trident.

Providing opposition during this training exercise was a single cohort of auxilia light infantry and two companies of cavalry. The commanding general's orders had been for them to harass the veterans of the First, subjecting them to the variety of hazards expected from the ever-elusive enemies in Britannia, who often refused to fight the Romans on their terms. While the infantry stood ready to harry the cohort with blunted throwing spears and arrows, a company of a hundred cavalrymen rode at a fast gallop in a wide arc around the left flank.

"*Hostiles on the left!*" an optio shouted.

"*Action left, set to repel cavalry!*" the man's centurion quickly ordered.

The century anchoring the left flank rapidly shifted to face the new threat, with legionaries in the first two ranks kneeling and planting their heavy javelins into the ground, forming a wall of spears. Those in the subsequent ranks hefted theirs to their shoulders, ready to throw. The centurion commanding the cavalry blew his whistle, and the horsemen rode at a canter back towards their companions. The legionaries reformed and continued to advance with the rest of the cohort. As they approached their objective, the auxilia skirmishers unleashed a volley of arrows and light throwing spears.

"*Testudo!*" centurions shouted.

Even in a wedge formation, legionaries were able to bring their shields to bear. Those in front dropped to one knee, hunkering down behind the protective wall. The rest hefted their shields overhead, forming a nearly impenetrable barrier from incoming missiles. The spears and arrows clattered off the encompassing shields. The men in front slowly stood, with the entire formation adjusting itself to close any gaps.

"*At the half-step... march!*"

That eight hundred men in a series of compressed formations could still manage to continue the advance, all the while being bombarded by a torrent of enemy missiles, was a testament to their training, experience, and discipline. It was but one of many formations that every last soldier in the First had drilled since his first days with the legion.

Watching the entire display was the Governor of Britannia, Publius Ostorius Scapula. A former legate, he had taken command of the Twentieth Legion soon after the initial conquest, four years prior. Following a standard three-year tour he returned to Rome. There he served for several months as suffect consul, before being dispatched back to Britannia. He was only the second man to attain the governorship of the province; the first being Aulus Plautius, the commander-in-chief of the initial invasion force. And while Emperor Claudius had been quick to declare victory following a series of decisive victories, the isle was anything but conquered. The lands under dominion of the Caesars only encompassed the south and southeast regions of Britannia. To the north was the vast Kingdom of the Brigantes. It was with good fortune that their queen, Cartimandua, was a strong Roman ally. They provided a buffer of sorts between Rome and the more hostile tribes further north. To the west, however, the people were anything but friendly. It was in these mountainous regions, beyond the River Sabrina, that their old enemy, Caratacus of the Catuvellauni, fled four years earlier. And it was into these treacherous lands that Scapula intended to unleash his army. If Britannia was truly to become part of the Roman Empire, then every last barbarian from Camulodunum in the east, all the way to Oceanus Atlanticus, would bow before the rule of the Caesars.

"The First Cohort still fights with the same discipline and tenacity as I remember," the governor said to the legion's current legate, a thirty-six year old general named Gaius Suetonius Paulinus. Scapula then added, "Of course you're used to dealing with elite troops. After all, wasn't it you who first successfully led an expedition over the Atlas Mountains in Mauretania?"

The legate grinned at the memory. "Yes, well, I think some of those lads were all brawn with little brain. There were many days when I felt a bit soft in the head myself for having attempted such a feat. These men here have a fine reputation, both in terms of valour and tactical savvy."

Paulinus nodded towards the ongoing skirmish, where the First Cohort continued to execute its drills with rapid precision. As they closed the distance, alternating ranks charged, while the rest unleashed their javelins simultaneously. It completely caught the auxilia infantry off-guard and they began to scatter.

The legate then remarked, "If the rest of the legion didn't have to spend so much time building roads and shovelling shit, the whole lot of them would become as proficient as the First."

"Yes, well, someone has to build the roads in this uncivilized land," the governor noted. "And you cannot have slaves doing it. Damn things would crumble within weeks if you did."

"I'm told the people of this isle make terrible slaves; too fiercely independent of mind."

"Bloody stubborn, more like," Scapula scoffed. "I honestly don't know who is more difficult to control, the Britons or those damned Jews in Judea."

Satisfied that the training had gone well, the governor excused himself and rode back towards the city, where his palace and administrative buildings all sat on what had once been the capital stronghold of their indigenous enemies, the Catuvellauni. Seeing that the First Cohort was almost finished with their drills, General Paulinus decided to firs have a word with the centurion primus pilus, before leaving to check on the progress of a bridge that was being constructed by one of the other cohorts. He would then return to the fortress to deal with the endless tedium of administrative issues that plagued every legate in command of an imperial legion.

The exercises finished to the master centurion's satisfaction, he blew his whistle, and all ceased brawling. Legionary and auxilia alike rested on their shields, removing helmets and wiping copious amounts of sweat from their faces and hair. The senior officer then turned each century over to its commander and left to have a word with the legate. The commander of the cohort's Third Century exhorted his men, giving them a few minor deficiencies to correct. He then dismissed his soldiers before removing his helmet and running his fingers through his hair, which was a thick mop of dark blonde. He walked with a slight limp, an old leg wound causing him much discomfort this day.

"I'm getting too old for this," he muttered.

His name was Magnus Flavianus. Like a growing number of imperial soldiers, his lineage was anything but Latin. Of Nordic ancestry, yet born in Ostia, just outside of Rome, his grandfather had won the family Roman citizenship as an auxilia soldier. Now fifty years old, Magnus had served in the ranks since he was seventeen. On days like this, the incessant throbbing in his leg, not to mention a plethora of other aches and dull pains, served as a harsh reminder to both his age, and to the savage decades he'd spent in service to the empire.

Even more painful was the knowledge that every last one of his friends from the early years was either dead or retired from the legions. His dearest friend, Artorius, who had had known for over thirty years, fighting side by side in Germania, Gaul, and even distant Judea, had left the army soon after the initial conquest of Britannia four years earlier. Artorius had been the centurion primus pilus of Legio XX, and had hoped, perhaps, his old friend would succeed him. Artorius refused to use his influence in the selection, however, and that promotion had gone to another.

"Magnus!"

The Norseman snapped out of his reverie and turned to see Master Centurion Tyranus, the very man who'd been promoted over him, walking briskly his way.

"I've briefed my men," the Norseman said, resting his leg atop a waist-high stone wall, trying to massage the pain away. "Optio Caelius and I will be overseeing a full kit inspection after supper."

"Good. And just so you know, we may be putting our training to use sooner rather than later."

"Who is it this time?" Magnus asked. "Surely our governor learned his lesson with the Iceni. When attempting to disarm an entire kingdom, an ally at that, one can only expect to be met with violent resistance."

Tyranus shook his head. "No, the Iceni are no longer an issue. Fortunately, King Prasutagus made Scapula see reason. He agreed to crucify the leaders of the revolt, provided he be allowed to keep his militias armed. Plus they will maintain their own security, negating the need for Roman troops on their soil."

"As long as they pay the required taxes every autumn, I don't see why we should bother with them. I have to say, I actually like Prasutagus, he's a rather affable fellow. Although, his wife, Boudicca, strikes me as an insufferable bitch."

Tyranus raised an eyebrow as he noted the centurion's rather pained expression. "By Juno, are you alright?"

"I'll be fine, just give me a few minutes."

The master centurion shook his head. "*Fine* is exactly what you are not. That old wound has been giving you much grief lately."

"It never healed properly," Magnus confessed glumly. "Artorius suffered almost the exact same injury once; except he was twenty-two at the time and in prime health. I was more than twice that age when that filthy barbarian got lucky."

"I remember that day well." Tyranus removed his helmet and leaned against the stone wall, his arms folded. "They said the fortress of Mai Dun was impregnable, yet we broke it in a day…" He stopped quickly, as Magnus winced at a pain unrelated to his leg. "I am sorry, old friend. I know not all wounds are those of the flesh."

"I stayed in the ranks to atone for my failure to save her. The pain I suffer every day is my punishment…" Magnus then shook his head quickly. "But enough of that. You didn't come here to discuss an old centurion's broken body and spirit. So tell me who we're putting our training to use against."

The primus pilus thought to express his concerns regarding Magnus' fitness for duty, but then thought better of it. "It's Caratacus," he said, causing the Norseman to perk up.

"Bugger me. So our old nemesis has returned."

"He never really left. He's been lying dormant for some time, gathering allies. After the Battle of the Twin Rivers, all of us thought the Catuvellauni threat was no more. King Togodumnus was slain along with thousands of their warriors. Hell, they surrendered their capital stronghold without a blow being struck! But Togodumnus' brother has always been a threat, stealing livestock, raiding border villages, kidnapping friendly nobles. That is, if the rumours are true."

"Do you believe them?"

"Whether it is Caratacus or not is of little concern," Tyranus stated. "What I do know is the tribes west of the Sabrina are causing havoc among our colonies. The Ordovices, Demetae, and Silures are the largest tribes in the region. They have been kept in check by constantly fighting amongst each other. However, if there is any validity to what Governor Scapula has heard, it would appear someone has brought them together."

Two hundred miles away near the mouth of the River Deva Fluvius, a small farming community lay in ruins. Thatched roofs burned, livestock were either dead or taken, bodies of both men and women alike lay strewn about. The survivors had been taken as slaves, hands bound, and all tied together in a long line. The raiders were well-known to them. The Silures were an unpredictable and extremely violent people who preferred brute force to negotiation. King Orin's brother, the previous king, was killed during the last war against Rome. Even now, there was only one way of dealing with his neighbours who aided the invaders.

As the shrieks of women and their children continued to echo, two warriors met near the smouldering hulk of what had once been the local chief's hall. One wore a hooded cloak, his face hidden in the shadow lest any survivors from the village recognize him. The other was the elusive man who stalwartly continued to lead the resistance against Rome these past four years. His name was Caratacus. Standing a half-head taller than most of his warriors, he was an imposing figure. His hair, which had before been kept long and braided, was now cropped short and spikey. His long moustache was showing traces of grey, with lines showing both age and endless strain forming along his brow and around his eyes. He wore a mail shirt, similar to the lorica hamata chainmail worn by Roman auxiliaries, with a multi-coloured cloak over his left shoulder. His broadsword, which he now ran an oil rag over, had witnessed countless battles.

"The latest blow against those who have become wilful slaves of Rome," he asserted to his companion, who nodded in concurrence. "A pity we had to slay so many of your people, but it had to be convincing."

"These people are nothing but slaves of fear, as is the bitch who rules over them."

Caratacus smiled appreciatively before reaching into his tunic and producing a gold torque. "A token of gratitude from King Orin."

The other warrior took the torque and turned it over in his hands. "Gold is a rarity in these isles," he said. "Yet the Silures possess plenty of it. Few have crossed into their lands, and these gifts of gold only add to their mystery."

"Do not worry about where the gold comes from," Caratacus said sternly. "Continue to show your gratitude by helping us undermine the alliance your cunt of a wife has formed with Rome."

The hooded warrior flashed an understanding grin. His name was Venutius, consort to Queen Cartimandua of the Brigantes; the largest kingdom in all Britannia. Yet instead of joining the alliance that Caratacus' brother, Togodumnus, had formed to repel the invaders, Cartimandua had offered her immediate submission to the armies of Caesar.

The queen's capitulation caused numerous rifts within the people of Brigantes. Venutius had attempted to take a band of warriors to join the resistance, but was overridden by his wife; a humiliating blow to his manhood and status as a great warrior. Even those who most hated the Romans were still loyal to their queen, as they had been to her father before. Four years later, those nostalgic feelings were beginning to fade, as Venutius and his allies continued in their subtle and subversive war of public opinion against the Romans, who continued to expand their territory even further into Britannia.

Following the ignominious defeat and death of Togodumnus, along with the subjugation of his people, the Brigantes consort had also feared his friend, Caratacus, was slain. Within the last year, however, the fugitive Catuvellauni prince made his presence known once more. And Venutius was only too glad to serve as a foil against his estranged wife, for it was he who arranged for the border village to be left undefended. Caratacus and his Silures allies had been allowed to sack the settlement, sending a message to all who would bow before a foreign emperor in distant Rome.

Unconcerned by the dead, even though they were his tribesmen, Venutius observed, "By bringing the people of the western mountains together, you have succeeded where so many have failed."

"The Silures played only a small role in the last war," Caratacus recalled. "Though their king, and a small band of his elite fighters, did stand with us in a show of solidarity. His death, while tragic, made the Roman threat painfully clear to all the Silures." He gave a short laugh. "Not that Orin minded becoming king after his brother's demise. He even took his pregnant sister-in-law as his queen."

"The Silures have a reputation for being the most fanatical fighters in all of Britannia," Venutius concurred. "However, they are a wild people and will be very difficult to control. And their numbers alone will not be enough to defeat the Romans."

Caratacus sheathed his sword. "Let me worry about the Silures. With my own people cowering before the Romans, Brigantes is now the largest kingdom in all the land. Only the Iceni have a comparable number of fighting men, and they have been squabbling of late with their imperial overlords."

"These raids will show my people that the protection of Rome is useless," Venutius surmised. Adding disdainfully, "Their queen will continue to supplicate herself before the emperor, leaving the citizens of Brigantes in want of a strong leader."

"Cartimandua is but a woman," Caratacus remarked, his frustration at Venutius' inability to control his own wife was a constant source of frustration. "How can you allow her to be all that stands in the way of us uniting against the invaders?"

"Because her father, King Breogan, inexplicably named his daughter as his sole heir, that she should rule Brigantes in her own right. I loved Breogan like he was my own father, but his short-sightedness regarding the succession was unforgiveable. Our people are divided regarding the Romans. Yet so long as the warrior classes hold onto the memory of their beloved king, there is little I can do, short of leading a rebellion against my own wife and queen."

"And that is what you may have to do." Caratacus glared harshly at him.

Venutius gritted his teeth.

"Despite the differences between our peoples, I have always considered you a friend and brother," he said. "Your children are as dear to me as if they were my own. And I mourned Togodumnus with you, while cursing the treason of your younger brother, Amminus. But these minor raids will not be enough to convince the people to turn against their queen. They will need to see the Romans themselves as vulnerable. We must draw them into invading the lands in the west, which they have thus far avoided. Defeat them. Win a decisive victory and my warriors will undoubtedly rise up, regardless of whether the queen is still Rome's docile bitch."

Chapter II: Shadows from the Past

The hill fort of Mai Dun (now known as Maiden Castle)

The echoes of battle were deafening. More than ten thousand imperial soldiers stormed the seemingly unassailable heights. The hill was steep and covered in tall grass, slick from the rains of the previous week. Catapults and ballistae bombarded the winding approach to the eastern gate of the ancient hill fort. Yet, for the vast majority of General Vespasian's army, their assault would simply be straight up into the teeth of enemy spear and blade.

Centurions and their subordinate officers shouted orders. The soldiers pulled themselves ever upward. Sling stones, light throwing spears, and the occasional arrow bombarded them as they tried to keep behind the protection of their shields. The bodies of the less fortunate, who had been struck in the face, neck, or legs, which were unprotected by their heavy armour, lay strewn along the slopes. The more gravely wounded cried out as they clutched at shattered limbs and torn flesh.

Surging upwards, the assailants came upon a large defilade that could not be seen from below. Encircling the entire hill, soldiers had to tumble down almost twenty feet before scaling back up the hill.

After another fifty-foot climb they came upon a second defilade. All the while, the barbarian skirmishers at the very top continued to bombard them relentlessly.

A centurion looked to the company of Syrian archers following his cohort. Their commander, a woman who had once fought in the arena, wordlessly nodded in agreement as the Roman officer pointed his gladius towards the heights. The cohort swarmed into this last defilade, while the Syrian archers fanned out and unleashed a salvo of arrows towards the defenders. The barbarian skirmishers began to fall, turning their attention away from the advancing legionaries and toward their immediate source of strife. Though outmatched in skill, they had the advantage of holding the high ground, as well as superior numbers. The Syrians' mail armour offered some protection, though it palled in comparison to the heavy plate worn by legionaries. Several were struck down by arrows and sling stones to the arms, legs, face, and neck, with heavier spears rupturing the light chain mail.

The fit and nubile woman leading the Roman allies was shouting words of encouragement to her fighters, pausing to let loose a series of her own arrows in rapid succession. Time then slowed. She saw the large spear flying in a high arc from the defences. Momentarily paralyzed, she was unable to leap away. The heavy blade burst through her armour, plunging deep into her stomach. Her cry of anguish was drowned out by the deafening din of battle. She fell to her knees, clawing frantically at the spear, as blood gushed from the hideous wound. Her tear-stained eyes gazing skyward, she quietly uttered, "Our child…my love, save us…*Magnus!*"

Magnus bolted upright, his face covered in sweat and his breathing coming in rapid gasps. It was the middle of the night. Despite the cool breeze blowing through the open window, he was hot, and his skin flushed. He took a deep breath and fought back the sobs that came in the aftermath of every such nightmare. Some nights he was able to suppress his sorrows, others he was not.

The same dream continued to haunt him since that terrible day during the assault of the barbarian hill fort at Mai Dun. For the Romans, the attack had been a moment of supreme triumph. General Vespasian's forces had broken the supposedly impenetrable stronghold in less than a day. Hundreds of slaves had been captured, with the local king slain. For his decisive victory, the legate had been awarded *triumphal regalia* by the Senate of Rome.

But for Centurion Magnus Flavianus, the death of his lover continued to plague him remorselessly. Every time the dream came, it was as if he were there, forced to watch, helpless as Achillia's guts were ripped open, killing her and their unborn child. In reality, though both Magnus and Achillia had taken part in the assault, they had been nowhere near each other. Magnus did not know she was dead until well after the battle was over. He himself had been gravely wounded. The horrific scarring and the incessant pain in his leg were an endless reminder of that dark day. In many ways it bound him to the terrible past, never allowing him to let his pain go. He could not count the number of times he'd cursed the gods for not taking him instead. He was a soldier of Rome, and it was more fitting that he should die, rather than his lover and their son or daughter, who would have been four years old.

Knowing sleep would be impossible to come by this night, the centurion threw on his cloak and stepped out into the cool night. The cold caused his muscles to tighten up, aggravating the ache in his leg. For this reason, he always rose well before any of the other officers, allowing himself time to work out the soreness and make his leg reasonably functional. Some of the men in his century wondered if he slept at all.

"It's been a while since we've been on an active campaign," a voice said behind him. Centurion Metellus appeared to be having a sleepless night of his own, as he too was taking a night-time stroll through the camp. Metellus Artorius Posthumous was the adopted son of Magnus' closest friend, Titus Artorius Justus. An accomplished soldier in his own right, Metellus was given command of the Fifth Cohort when Tyranus was elevated to centurion primus pilus.

"Is that why you can't sleep?" Magnus asked.

"I suppose it is," Metellus confessed. "Marcia worries every spring that I'll be sent off to get disembowelled by the barbarians that infest this land. Having time to watch my boys grow has made the consequences of being sent on campaign all the more stark. When I became a father, I realized it was no longer simply about me."

21

Magnus understood. The younger centurion had married a couple of years prior to the invasion of Britannia. His sons, Lucius and Gaius, were infants when the invasion force landed on these shores. They had since grown into a pair of energetic, precocious young lads.

"Marcia's fears may be well-founded this time," the Norseman conjectured. "It would seem some of our old enemies do not know when they've been conquered."

"So I heard. We have yet to venture into the lands of the Silures, yet I think Scapula won't have much of a choice if these raids continue. They've been harrying the Brigantes, hoping to goad them into breaking their alliance with us."

"A handful of survivors have stated they were led by our old friend, Caratacus," the older centurion recalled.

"I think they were set loose on purpose," Metellus added. "Caratacus wants us to know he's behind these attacks. We may have killed his brother and taken their lands, but there will never be peace in Britannia so long as he lives."

"They want a war but on their own terms." Magnus shook his head. "From what I understand, the lands west of the River Sabrina are extremely mountainous and full of hostile barbarians, not just the Silures. I believe this campaign will be about more than capturing or killing Caratacus. Scapula has to know that, while we have the Brigantes to the north, we must expand Roman Britannia all the way to the western sea. Otherwise, our provincials will never sleep safely at night."

Centurion Magnus was not alone in his sleeplessness, nor was Metellus the only one concerned for his family. For Caratacus, though his people may have submitted to the emperor, he would not have his children raised as Roman slaves. It was for their freedom, and that of their future children, that he had returned to fight the imperial invaders. And on this particular night, his trepidation for his family was tempered by hatred, brought on by an old betrayal.

Unbeknownst to the Romans, the Catuvellauni prince had eyes in many corners of Britannia, especially in the south. Caratacus himself had once conquered the Kingdom of Atrebates whose king, a Roman ally, fled to Rome and begged Emperor Claudius to liberate them. Thus began the Invasion of Britannia. The imperial scum now sought to control the entire isle, while placing their own lapdog on the Atrebates throne. And it was Caratacus' spies within the court of King Cogidubnus who brought him the hateful news regarding the return of a man he once loved.

"My brother has returned to despoil the land of our ancestors," he said, forcing himself to contain his wrath. He ran his sharpening stone over his sword, as he did on many nights when vexations prevented sleep. His wife, Eurgain, sat beside him and wrapped her arms around his shoulders.

"Amminus?" she asked. "He has not been seen in these lands for ten years. I thought he was dead."

Caratacus slowly shook his head, his gaze ever fixed on the dancing flames. "No, he ran like a whipped dog to Caesar, soon after our father removed him as ruler of the Cantiaci. He'd hoped the Romans would give him those lands back. Instead, he is little more than a courtier to that bastard, Cogidubnus, who now rules over half the lands of our people; lands which I had conquered."

"You know this...how?"

The old war chief grinned, never averting his stare from his blade, which reflected the glowing fire light. "We lost our homes when Togodumnus gave his life for our ungrateful people, yet we still have many friends in these isles. And my scouts also tell me the Roman governor grows exasperated with the raids from our friends, the Silures. He is planning to invade the western mountains. They will swallow up his legions, and I shall avenge our family."

"And what of our son?" Eurgain asked. "He comes of age soon. Will you allow him to stand with his father in battle?"

"Jago has proven his bravery, growing up in the shadow of the oppressors. But he is even younger than I was, when my father had this sword forged for me by our finest smiths. I would protect him from having to draw blade against the Romans, but I fear our son will have to become a man far sooner than I did."

Eurgain clasped her husband's forearm. "If Jago is not ready, let me take his place," she pleaded. "It is not unheard of for the women of this land to take up arms and fight beside their men. I am skilled with both spear and sword. You *know* this! And what other duty has a mother but to protect her children?"

23

Caratacus finally diverted his eyes from the now-dying flames and looked into the hard gaze of his wife. "You were indeed well-named, *Eurgain—strength of the bear*. But what should happen to Jago, let alone our dearest little daughter, should both of us fall? Sorcha has scarcely seen her sixth winter, and I will not risk her losing father and mother."

Caratacus stood and sheathed his sword. He walked quietly over to a low shelter of animal hides where both his children slept. The top of Sorcha's head was barely visible, as she lay curled up beneath a large bear skin blanket. Jago lay on his side, his face towards the fire, snoring quietly. Though well-grown for his age, he was still a boy of twelve, a full three years younger than Caratacus when he saw his first battle. And even then, his father, King Cunobeline, had thought his middle son was too young. It had been Togodumnus who convinced their father to let Caratacus prove his worth on the battlefield.

He gritted his teeth at the memory of his dear brother. And yet if Jago were to share his uncle's fate, so be it; all he asked of the gods was that he live to reach his full measure and fight as a true warrior of the Catuvellauni.

"Time," Caratacus said, gazing into the star-filled heavens. "I need more time with him."

The burning of villages and the slaying of her people had been deeply troubling for Queen Cartimandua. She had ordered a contingent of mounted warriors to patrol the region west of the River Sabrina. However, the terrain was far too mountainous, and they simply lacked the numbers to effectively combat the large bands of Ordovices and Silures warriors that infested the hills. The Brigantes queen had therefore dispatched one of her most trusted advisors to implore their imperial allies to come to their aid with all haste. Summer was fast approaching, and Cartimandua feared it would be almost fall by the time the legions marched across Britannia to address the raids into allied Brigantes. Though she retained her strong, stoic demeanour at court, the queen was becoming desperate. There had been whispers in all corners of the kingdom that she was weak, and the Romans were willing to let them be slaughtered. The number of dissidents was growing and becoming more vocal about their distaste for the alliance Queen Cartimandua forged with the empire.

It was unseasonably warm this spring day as Alaric, the most trusted member of the queen's court, rode into the Roman fortress at Camulodunum. A well-built man of Germanic stock, he was now in his mid-thirties. He had also seen more of the greater world than any man in all Britannia. As a young boy in Germania, he and his mother fled across the Britannic Sea, escaping the empire's onslaught during the wars between Arminius and the Roman imperial prince, Germanicus Caesar. Alaric had been raised in the house of Cartimandua's father, and the future Queen of Brigantes had looked after him like an elder sister.

Years later, and with much bitter irony, Alaric became an oarsman for the imperial navy, even fighting alongside his one-time enemies during a long and rather traumatic voyage to the remote province of Judea. It was in that hot and arid land that he found it within himself to forgive the Romans. This was in no small part due to the words of a Jewish teacher, who taught that one should love their enemies as well as their friends. Though this man was later crucified by the Romans, ostensibly for causing sedition and a potential uprising, his words remained close to the heart of the young man from Germania.

Alaric finally returned to Britannia, after being gone for the better part of twenty years, just prior to the Roman invasion. Queen Cartimandua welcomed him back by making him a member of her inner council. Though she later arranged a suitable marriage for him, with his wife bearing him two fine sons and a pair of beautiful daughters, it was the queen who still held his love. He would do anything for Cartimandua, without question; and so, when she asked him to act as her emissary to Ostorius Scapula, he did not hesitate. Accompanying him was an old childhood friend named Landon, who served as a captain within the queen's guard.

It took them several days to reach the city, which had changed drastically in appearance since being claimed as the imperial capital for Roman Britannia. The social classes and ethnicities had also started to change. Merchants and magistrates from the continent, most of whom dressed far differently than the natives, now lived side by side with the indigenous tribesmen. And even amongst the Catuvellauni, a large number of their wealthier nobles had adopted styles of Roman dress and grooming, with many of the men cutting their hair short and shaving their faces smooth.

"It is a strange thing," Alaric said as they rode towards the gate of the walled city. "That people across the world, who bear no resemblance to Rome, yet they seek to become just like them. I have seen cities in the hot wastelands of the east, where the dark-skinned people will dress and act like Romans. To think that eight hundred years ago, they were little more than a small village, not unlike ours, nestled among a series of hills."

"Hold!" a sentry said, interrupting their conversation and barring the way with his spear. "What brings you to Camulodunum?"

"An emissary of Queen Cartimandua with a message for the noble governor, Ostorius Scapula," Alaric replied.

"Leave your horses and any weapons here," the other sentry replied, taking the horse's bridle.

The two Brigantes men gazed around the inside of the city that was once capital of the Catuvellauni. The people still went about their daily lives, the majority caring little that it was a Roman governor who now lorded over them rather than their native king. Those who were most anti-Roman had fled long before the legions arrived. And while most of the structures were the traditional huts with thatched roofs, a small number of foreign-looking buildings stood out in stark contrast. These were large tile-roofed villas, each enclosed by a brick wall, belonging to either merchants or imperial administrators. Women in sheer togas, split up the side, plied their trade just outside the brothels. There were also two massive legionary fortresses just beyond the walls of the city, and Camulodunum was crawling with soldiers. Most were either messengers or officers with business for the governor, though there were the occasional bands of armoured legionaries patrolling the streets.

The governor's mansion and administrative building sat atop a small rise. The Catuvellauni king's great hall had been razed to the ground, with the majestic Roman palace erected over the remains. The guards on either side of the gate wore the segmented plate armour of legionaries, as opposed to the mail shirts worn by the gruffer looking auxiliaries who'd escorted Alaric into the city.

26

"A messenger from Queen Cartimandua," the trooper said.

"We'll take him from here. Return to your post." The decanus in charge of the palace's front gate waved for Alaric to follow him.

A mob of administrators, local chieftains, and various magistrates stood or sat on stone benches outside the governor's office, waiting their turn to see him. The soldiers forced their way through, causing much irritation and a few choice profanities. The squad leader knocking on the large door before opening it and peering in.

"Beg your pardon, governor, but there's a messenger here from Queen Cartimandua." He then looked back at Alaric and nodded his head towards the room. "You may enter."

Ostorius Scapula sat behind a large oak desk. A pair of freedman clerks sat on either end, taking notes and keeping track of the various piles of reports and correspondence. Seated across from him were two men in military tunics. Alaric guessed them to be legion commanders. The governor's eyes looked tired, as if he hadn't slept in days. It seemed as if lording over a province, particularly one as new and volatile as Britannia, was causing him much anxiety.

"And what word from our ally, the queen?" he asked, leaning back in his chair and wiping his eyes. "More Ordovices raids from across the Sabrina?"

The two legates turned their attention towards the messenger.

"These are not simple raiding parties," Alaric stated. "Nor is it just the Ordovices crossing into our lands. The Silures have come from the south in large numbers. My queen has sent mounted patrols across the river in an attempt to thwart further incursions, yet our enemies are simply too numerous for our warriors to contend with."

One of the legates, Suetonius Paulinus, spoke up. "I thought the Silures and Ordovices were mortal enemies."

"They are," Alaric acknowledged. "Or at least they were. King Orin of the Silures has little love for his neighbours to the north, yet someone has managed to unite them."

Scapula nodded thoughtfully. "And there is only one man, that we know of, who is charismatic enough to bring such generational rivals together to fight in a common cause."

"Caratacus," Paulinus said, echoing what every man in the room thought. "What of the other peoples in the region?"

27

"There is the Deceangli, whose territory is the strip of land along the north coast," Alaric answered. "They are really little more than a client state under the dominion of the Ordovices. One could say the same of the Demetae and Gangani to the far west. They are mostly fishermen, who supply the Silures with most of their boats."

"Should we have reason to fear an amphibious attack on our territories?" the legate of Legio IX, Lucius Paetus, asked.

"Fishing vessels make for poor warships," Scapula surmised. He then waited for Alaric to continue his message from Cartimandua.

"My queen implores Rome to send reinforcements as soon as possible. There has been much strife at court between her and the consort, Venutius. This has led to instability within our kingdom, which is why she cannot do more to fight this threat from the west. The queen fears if she commits too many of our warriors to fighting against Caratacus, Venutius may cause further trouble. She fears he may one day attempt to seize the throne."

"A family squabble within a barbarian kingdom," Paetus muttered, his voice full of contempt.

"That '*barbarian kingdom*' has been one of our most dependable allies," Paulinus rebuked before the governor could respond. "They are also the largest tribal people within Britannia. Should Cartimandua be overthrown, there is no telling what mischief Venutius could cause for Rome. We have enough trouble as it is dealing with those provincials under our control. Let us not forget, this land has only been Roman for four years. And if we're now having to deal with hostile tribes to the west, the last thing we need is a huge hostile army to the north. It would be fucking anarchy, and we would lose everything."

Scapula ignored the disagreement between his two legates. "If these are no mere raids, then why have they not seized any territory? Why do they cross back over the Sabrina?"

"I think it is provocation," the messenger replied. "They want a decisive battle against Rome. But they also want it on ground of their choosing."

"Revenge," Paulinus surmised. "The Silures may seek retribution for the death of their previous king, but the Ordovices could give a damn. After all, they took no part in the previous war. That tells me it is most likely Caratacus who has united them."

28

The governor remarked, "I suspect Caratacus, or whoever is behind these raids, also has spies in every corner of Roman Britannia. We should find alternate ways of reaching Silures, rather than simply walking all the way across Britannia."

"What do you have in mind?" Paetus asked.

Scapula grinned, his eyes still fixed on Alaric. "The Silures may not have a viable fleet readily available, but we do."

As Alaric and Landon made ready to leave, Paulinus halted them with a question. "Do either of you speak Silures?"

Chapter III: Brothers' Reunion and an Emperor's Lament

Camulodunum, Roman Capital of Britannia
June, 48 A.D.

Emperor Claudius

Despite the dire plea from Queen Cartimandua, there was much speculation within the magisterial circles and local nobility, as to whether the Romans could launch a viable assault against Caratacus that year. Governor Scapula had committed two of the province's four legions to the campaign, along with an equal number of auxilia infantrymen, plus several regiments of cavalry. The logistics involved in feeding and supplying over twenty-thousand men and all of their horses and pack animals was astronomical. The journey itself could be completed in two to three weeks; however, that still left a very short campaign season once they crossed into enemy held territory.

Scapula had sent a dispatch to Rome, making his objectives clear. His intent was not to just punish the Ordovices and Silures but to begin a fresh series of conquests, with the long-term objective of expanding Roman dominion all the way to the west coast. This had been met with great enthusiasm by Emperor Claudius as well as the consuls, Aulus Vitellius and Messalla Gallus. The Britannic fleet based out of the southern port of Portus Adurni was tasked with providing sufficient ships for his army. Legio IX, along with half the auxilia infantry and most of the cavalry, would make the journey by land. The remainder would take to the seas, sailing around southern Britannia and landing on the Deceangli coast. Scapula's intent was to trap Caratacus between his two divisions. Failing that, both his legates advised him to wrest control of the coastal regions held by the Deceangli and establish the army's winter camp there.

It was now mid-June. Just off the River Stour at Camulodunum, the capital of Roman Britannia, the naval assault forces began to assemble. Scapula had dispatched his land division, under the command of General Paetus, a few days prior. The governor himself would accompany General Paulinus and the Twentieth Legion. Since neither he nor any of his men had the slightest inclination what the terrain along the Deceangli coast looked like, he selected the lightest and most mobile auxilia infantry to accompany the maritime division. Due to the limited space aboard the imperial warships, he was only able to take a single regiment of cavalry. For this, he chose the venerable *Indus' Horse*.

"For all we know, the north coast could be as mountainous as the rest of the region," he said to General Paulinus as they watched the large flotilla of Roman warships make its way up the river.

Legio XX erected its temporary marching camp just off the river, with the auxilia encampments following along the Stour for several miles.

"I think we should have brought more than just a single regiment of cavalry," the legate remarked.

"Believe me, I wanted to," the governor replied. "However, the channel fleet only has five vessels capable of transporting horses, and two of these are in dry dock for repairs. Still, *Indus' Horse* is one of the finest regiments in the whole of the empire. Their record of service during the invasion was exemplary. I know they will fight well."

There was still much work to be done before the division could depart. The fleet admiral, Tiberius Stoppello, would need to be fully briefed on where he was expected to take such a vast portion of his ships. Contingency plans would have to be made, in case inclement weather ran the ships ashore or any changes needed to be made as to where the assault force would land. There was also the matter of making certain sufficient food stores were available and could be transported by Stoppello's ships. Given the massed quantities of rations needed to feed and imperial army, the concept of foraging was simply not practical. Therefore, the grain stores of the legionary fortresses and auxilia forts were emptied into thousands of sacks and placed aboard wagons. The shipment of regular resupplies of food and needed equipment would need to be coordinated with the fleet.

Not far away, Centurion Magnus and the rest of the First Cohort watched the ships gliding up the vast inlet of the river. The Britannic fleet was large and the Norseman guessed at least twenty warships were making their way toward the rendezvous point.

He then recognized the large red standard that flew from the back of the massive flagship. "Well, I'll be damned."

"You recognize them?" Tyranus asked.

"That's Admiral Stoppello's flag," Magnus explained. "We fought those pirates together during our journey to Judea. By Neptune, it's been seventeen years now."

"I remember him now," the primus pilus recalled. "He commanded the fleet that ferried us across the sea during the invasion."

The ships' commanders soon came ashore, along with the fleet admiral, to meet with Governor Scapula and General Paulinus. This would be the only face-to-face meeting they would have before the landing, in addition to being the first time the naval officers heard the details as to their destination. In addition to supply issues, there was the simple matter of sorting out which units would ride aboard which ships. It was crucial to both economise space, as well as prepare for enemy resistance once they reached the Deceangli coast.

Since the First Cohort of Legio XX was by far the largest element, and given their status as the elite troops of the division, it was assumed they would ride aboard Stoppello's flagship. Magnus walked along the shoreline, hoping to have a moment to greet the man who had shared in some of his more harrowing adventures. There were dozens of mariners mooring the ships, while their officers disembarked; however, Magnus reckoned the admiral would be easy to spot. He was very tall for a Sicilian and completely bald. The Nordic centurion's thoughts were interrupted by a bellowing voice coming from a sailor of the second ship.

"By Thor's hammering cock!"

Before Magnus could turn to see the source of the voice, a large mass tackled him to the ground, knocking the wind from his lungs. Magnus struggled to throw his assailant off him. He flipped onto his back, eyes rolling for a moment as he recognized his brother. Hansi Flavianus was commander of the second ship in the line and, perhaps, the only man in the entire division large enough to manhandle the Norse centurion. Legionary and sailor alike were watching the spectacle in both bemusement and confusion.

"Oh, sorry, little brother. I forget the army has made you soft after all these years." Hansi was taller than Magnus, with an equally thick mop of blonde hair atop his head. In Roman fashion, he was also clean-shaven. Though two years older, his face seemed ageless. As he stood up, he leaned down and offered his hand, laughing all the while.

Magnus gritted his teeth, and while still trying to force air back into his lungs, punched his fist hard into his brother's groin. Hansi doubled over, falling onto his shoulder.

"Nicely done," he wheezed, clutching his manhood. He gasped and pulled himself up, suddenly aware of hundreds of eyes staring at them. With great annoyance in his voice he barked, *"Alright, no one told you to stop working!"*

"I'll be buggered," Magnus laughed, shaking his head and embracing his brother. "I thought for certain the fell beasts of Neptune had swallowed you up by now."

"Only thing getting swallowed by fell beasts is my cock!" his brother roared with laughter. "I've been wondering ever since they gave us this assignment, what are the chances that my baby brother is still with the legions? To be honest, I'm kind of surprised you're alive. Last I heard, you were bleeding your guts out on the slopes of some barbarian hill fort."

"They got me in the leg, not my guts," Magnus corrected, showing Hansi the scar.

"Nice one. Surely the gods will let you into Valhalla with a mark like that." With his arm around Magnus' shoulder, they walked toward the assembling officers.

"And what of you?" Magnus asked. "How many more years do you plan on splashing about on your little boat?"

"There's nothing for me back home," Hansi replied. "I figure I'll keep sailing until the seas claim my corpse or the emperor decides he has no more use for me. Lucky for me, he's giving me a whole mess of boats to play with soon."

"You're taking over the Britannic fleet?"

Hansi shook his head. "No. Stoppello is like me; he's not ready to give this life up just yet, the selfish old bastard. He's recommended I assume command the Tyrrhenian fleet out of Ostia, and the senate has accepted."

"Ostia," Magnus mused. "So I guess that means you are going home after all."

He shrugged. "More or less. Though they always talked about keeping a strong bond with our ancestral lands in the Norse lands, Father and Grandfather raised us to be Romans. Ostia is more home to me than some balls-freezing land where I've never even been. But that may change..." His voice trailed off for a brief moment.

Before Magnus could inquire what his last words meant, Hansi began again. "Best part about getting the Tyrrhenian fleet is the flagship; it's an Octeres-class behemoth. Eight files of a hundred oarsmen on each side, sixteen-hundred total. Plus another thousand sailors and marines. It cuts through the seas at great speed, and is remarkably manoeuvrable for a ship of that size. A true fortress of the seas, and soon she will be mine!"

They soon arrived at the meeting place, and Magnus was obligated to join his fellow senior officers from Legio XX. However, there was something he wanted to know first.

"You say the senate approved your promotion to admiral," he said. "I always thought such a posting came directly from the emperor."

"Yes, well..." Hansi paused for a moment. "Obviously none of you have been told about the little problems within the imperial family as of late. I'll give you the details later, but suffice it to say, Emperor Claudius had far more important issues to deal with than the posting of a single flag officer in the fleet. To be quite honest, he's fortunate he still has his skin, let alone remain Caesar."

"It is done, Caesar," Narcissus, the emperor's freedman, said solemnly.

Claudius lounged on his dining couch, his eyes distant as he slowly drained his wine chalice, his fourth in the last half hour. The emperor gave an almost imperceptible nod of acknowledgment and held out his hand. Narcissus gave him the report, which detailed the execution of Empress Valeria Messalina. Her lover, the consul-designate, Gaius Silius, would be executed by strangulation atop the Gemonian Stairs the following afternoon. Fellow conspirators had confessed that they intended to overthrow the emperor, with Silius becoming regent for Messalina's son, Britannicus. Despite this vile treason, Claudius could not bring himself to have his wife, whom he'd loved with every last measure of his very soul, subjected to the humiliation of a public execution.

Messalina and Silius had been carrying on an affair for almost a year; albeit Silius was just the latest in a string of lovers the empress had taken into her bed over the years. It seemed everyone in Rome, except the emperor, knew of her rampant promiscuity. She was renowned within in the brothels, where she had volunteered her 'services' in an effort to satisfy her endless lust. Rumour had it she had once competed against a legendary prostitute to see who could wear out the most men in a day...and won.

"I c...could have forgiven her infidelities," the emperor said quietly, more to himself than to his freedman. "What could I have done to drive her away? She was all I have ever loved..."

"They planned to *murder* you, Caesar," Narcissus replied firmly.

Of course, the emperor knew this. Were there any doubts as to Messalina's guilt, he never would have signed the order for her execution.

"Her farce of a marriage to Silius was to humiliate and weaken you. Had they succeeded in escaping justice, your head—and mine most likely   would be on a spike. Silius would now be attempting to seize the throne for himself, under the false pretence of serving as regent for your son. It's all there in his confession."

"My son," Claudius whispered, shaking his head. Given the sheer volume of Messalina's adulteries, could he even be sure Britannicus was his son? And what of the lad's elder sister, Octavia?

Was she the emperor's daughter or the spawn from one of her mother's random liaisons?

A long, awkward silence followed. Narcissus sympathized deeply with Claudius, who was as much a personal friend as he was his emperor. Up until a day ago, he'd been very much in love with his young wife, not knowing she had been humiliating him openly while plotting his overthrow and death.

The sound of hobnailed sandals echoing on the floor tiles down the hall brought both men out of their contemplative reverie. They were soon joined by the praetorian prefect, Lucius Geta. He was accompanied by a centurion named Cornelius, whose blade slain the empress. Cornelius was one of the praetorians who saved Claudius' life after the murder of his nephew, Emperor Gaius Caligula, seven years before. He also helped Claudius attain the imperial throne soon after. As such, the emperor was very fond of him. He took it as a sign of Cornelius' devout loyalty that he was willing to kill his empress. Little did he know, Messalina was responsible for the death of the centurion's wife. This killing was as much about vengeance as duty.

"Empress of Death," the prefect said, breaking the silence. "At least that's what some of the lads called her." What he did not say was that many of his soldiers further stated she carried death both in her viper's tongue, as well as between her legs.

"Despite her crimes, I still hoped she would have the dignity to end her own life," the emperor mused. Now on his fifth chalice of wine, he was relaxing substantially and feeling more accepting of what he'd had to do.

"She lacked any sense of dignity, Caesar," Cornelius said coldly. Given his history with the emperor, the centurion often spoke more candidly towards him than most men of his rank and status. "Strangulation atop the Gemonian Stairs would have been fitting."

"We captured over two hundred people at her 'wedding' to Silius," Geta added quickly, casting a glare over at his centurion. "What's to be done with them?"

Narcissus pondered for a moment and said, "I recommend we determine which are the lowest-born and, therefore, of little to no threat. Have them exiled with all their lands and fortunes confiscated. It would look rather despotic if we spent the next week piling up the bodies on the Gemonian Stairs."

"Agreed," the prefect concurred. He turned to the emperor. "The people still recall the bloodbath your Uncle Tiberius left in the wake of Sejanus' betrayal. Let them see justice, not tyranny."

Narcissus nodded in consent. "Those closest to Messalina will have to be put to death, naturally. Thankfully, they only amount to a handful."

"See to it," Claudius said, dismissively waving his hand.

The men all bowed and began to leave the dining hall.

"Cornelius!" the emperor called out.

"Yes, Caesar?"

"I…if I ever decide to get married again, p…promise you'll run me through with your sword."

It was a rain-soaked morning when the Britannic fleet set sail from Camulodunum. Legionaries, who were mostly confined to the topside, huddled beneath their thick traveling cloaks as they were pummelled by both rain and sea spray. Despite the terrible weather, there were still plenty of ships making their way to and from the isle. The majority of merchant vessels from the continent came via a pair of ports in northern Gaul. The largest, Gesoriacum, was where the initial invasion of Britannia had been staged. Ships coming from Gesoriacum were mostly bound for the River Tamesis, which would take them to the growing city of Londinium. Doubtless the numerous merchant ships and fishing boats would spread the word of a large-scale Roman operation, once they saw the fleet of ships crammed full of legionaries and auxilia troopers. Magnus said as much to his brother as they watched a trio of fishermen staring at them wide-eyed. The wake from the large warships rocked their small boat.

"It can't be helped," Hansi remarked with a shrug. "By nightfall, everyone in Cantiaci and Atrebates will know we are up to something. But even if Caratacus still has friends in those regions, by the time they get word to him, you'll have long since landed and begun slapping around the Ordovices a bit."

"How many days did Admiral Stoppello say it would take to reach our destination?"

His brother furrowed his brow and thought for a few moments. "He wasn't exactly sure, since none of us have ever been there. Though my best guess would be four, maybe five. We'll reach Vectis Island before the end of the day. It will take another day to round the southwest peninsula which will take us to Silures territory. Stoppello will likely keep us just beyond sight of the shoreline, lest the Silures sound the alarm. Unfortunately, none of us have been further north than where the River Sabrina feeds into the sea."

"So none of you have ever seen the legendary isle the locals call Hibernia?" Magnus asked.

"If only," his brother chuckled. "Rumour has it the Brigantes control much of the eastern regions, though apparently Queen Cartimandua will neither confirm nor deny this. Hell, I'm not certain the isle even exists."

The weather was known to change very rapidly in southern Britannia, and even more so along the channel sea. A couple of hours after their departure, the rains ceased, leaving just a light misting in the air. By late afternoon the sun shone brightly. The soldiers threw off their cloaks and enjoyed the warm summer day. As the fleet approached Vectis Island, the ships veered to the north, sailing through the waters known as *The Solent.*

"Look lads!" the sailing master shouted from the ship's forecastle, *"there's home!"*

"Seems like we just left," a sailor muttered.

"Portus Adurni," Hansi explained to his brother. "I know it's just a collection of ramshackle buildings and a fishing village, but the natural harbour and centralized location makes it the ideal headquarters for the fleet. A pity I won't be around to see if they ever build a decent fort here."

As the setting sun glared in their faces, the ships anchored for the night near a rather unusual harbour. The isle seemed to end, with the exception of a long, narrow sandbar that extended a couple miles to the south, connecting to a small island. Magnus stood along the ship's railing, staring towards the mainland.

"You know where we are?" Hansi asked.

His brother nodded.

"Achillia and I spent an evening along this sandy beach, just prior to the attack on Mai Dun."

Though the hillfort was perhaps eight or ten miles from the shore, neither man could actually see it due to the rolling hills, high hedgerows, and large expanses of trees.

Magnus nodded towards the sandbar. "Though I did not realize it at the time, it was here that I spent the happiest night of life."

Chapter IV: Delivered by Neptune

Halkyn Mountain, Deceangli Territory
Mid-June 48 A.D.

Roman Legionary

Though he had no knowledge of the fleet manoeuvring around the coast, word of the other Roman column's advance across Britannia reached Caratacus within a few days. The former Catuvellauni prince summoned a meeting of his allies atop a formidable hill he was claiming as his temporary stronghold.

King Orin of the Silures came with a thousand of his best warriors. Their curled hair and darker complexion denoted their Iberian ancestry, in stark contrast to the light skinned and more fair-haired indigenous tribes. Since the Romans sullied the lands of the Catuvellauni, the Silures had become Caratacus' closest allies. Orin often called him 'brother'; their bond growing stronger with each battle fought against the invaders. As the king had no sons or other living male relatives, there was rumour he intended to name Caratacus as his heir. A noble gesture that would prove unlikely to ever come to fruition, as Caratacus was several years older than the Silures king.

King Seisyll of Ordovices had arrived with five hundred of his personal guardsmen. Like the Silures, the Ordovices were not native to Britannia. They emigrated from northern Germanic and Nordic lands nearly five hundred years before. They were much larger and fairer-skinned than their neighbours to the south. While they were certainly valiant in battle, they lacked the bloodthirsty, ever-supressed rage that seemed to course through the veins of every Silures warrior.

Eurgain stood with her husband, in awe that a foreign exiled prince, whose lands now belonged to the Romans, had succeeded in compelling these age-old enemies to unite.

"King Orin," Seisyll said with a nod. "By the grace of our friend, the noble Caratacus, I bid you welcome to my people's lands."

"And I accept," Orin replied, as the two clasped forearms. "Let us go forward as allies from this day against our common enemy."

"My brothers," Caratacus said, his arms raised high, "it is with much joy and hope for all our peoples that I see the two mightiest tribes in this land united under a common cause. Our raids have been effective in cowering the Brigantes, and the Romans have taken the bait. That simpering bitch, Cartimandua, grovels before her masters, begging them for aid."

"They are the largest kingdom in all of Britannia, yet they cower before our warriors," Seisyll said with a derisive grin.

"How soon until our weapons taste their flesh?" Orin asked.

"Soon," Caratacus reassured him. "Before the next ten sunrises the armies of Caesar will cross over the River Sabrina. Their forces number no more than ten thousand fighting men; a single legion, a few cohorts of auxilia infantry, and several regiments of cavalry."

Seisyll remarked, "They are either bold or foolish, if they think they can subdue us with such a pathetic force. My warriors alone significantly outnumber them."

"The woods will soon devour their flesh," Caratacus continued. "And the mountains will grind their bones into dust."

A great feast was held that night. Copious amounts of mead and ale were consumed, with boars, deer, and other game roasted on giant spits. The warriors present were all members of the royal households, and their behaviour was measurably more subdued than that of the common rabble. However, both Silures and Ordovices

41

alike engaged in feats of strength as well as outright brawls, while their kings looked on and enjoyed the spectacle.

"I hope they save some of their rage for the Romans," Seisyll said to his peer from Silures.

"My people live to fight," Orin replied. "Though I confess, it is better that their rage is focused on the imperial invaders rather than our northern neighbours." There was a sinister trace to his words.

Seisyll paid it no mind. The Silures were an extremely aggressive and warlike race; however, this also meant they were difficult for even their beloved king to lord over. King Orin, like his brother before him, had kept their people in a constant state of conflict lest they fall into anarchy and fighting amongst each other. Only the strongest of hands could control the Silures. Yet Orin was slowly beginning to see there was one even stronger than he who could do so. As Caratacus joined the kings, he passed a jug of mead between them. The men drank to their health, to the glory of their ancestors, the valour of their collective warriors, and the obliteration of the imperial menace.

"There it is," Stoppello said, pointing to the large river mouth several miles distant.

Neither Governor Scapula nor General Paulinus could quite see it; however, they trusted the admiral's superior vision. The fleet had formed into a long line, with the distant shore off to their right. As the fog broke, Paulinus was able to see the large sandbar that dominated the landscape. Just beyond the beach the ground rose up to what looked like a small ridge in the distance.

"The terrain here looks relatively flat," he observed. "It's not as rugged and broken as the southern regions."

"And there's a nice beach for us," Scapula said to Stoppello. "We'll land here."

Stoppello called out over his shoulder, *"Signal the fleet...action right! All assault troops make ready to debark!"*

"That would be us, lads!" Master Centurion Tyranus shouted to his men. "First Cohort, up!"

Anticipating the pending debarkation, all legionaries had been ordered into their armour and kit just before dawn. Soldiers donned their helmets and stood ready, using their shields and pila to help balance themselves.

"This area appears to be deserted," Paulinus said to his primus pilus. The ship lurched hard to the right as oarsmen cut into the waves, training the ship towards the shore. "Once off the ship, press forward to that rolling ridge. It looks to be about a mile inland and should make a good staging point."

"Yes, sir."

Centurion Magnus leaned against his shield, as the ship cut through the rolling surf. He tied the helmet cords beneath his chin and took a deep breath in anticipation. He clenched his fist and beat it hard against the scar on his leg, drawing a bemused stare from Optio Caelius.

"Trying to wake the damn thing up," the Norseman explained.

"I didn't say a thing, sir," Caelius said with an understanding grin. The optio had his share of scars and old injuries, and could therefore sympathise with his commanding officer.

"Four fathoms!" a sailor at the stern of the ship shouted, as he pulled in the long knotted roped used for estimating depth.

"Stand ready, lads," Magnus said. He hefted his shield. "Just a little further."

"The cohort will advance in column until we reach the beach!" Master Centurion Tyranus shouted. "At my signal, we will form into battle ranks!"

"Three fathoms!"

Magnus scanned the horizon, anxiously looking for enemy warriors. There was little doubt they had been spotted during the previous day's voyage. The only question now was whether or not hostile forces would be waiting for them on the other side of the ridge.

"Two fathoms!"

"Stand by to reverse oars!" Admiral Stoppello ordered.

Magnus could now see the sandy bottom beneath the waves. He took a deep breath and slung his shield over the railing. Many of his legionaries followed suit as they prepared to jump over the side.

"One-and-a-half fathoms!"

"Reverse and withdraw oars!"

Orders were shouted below deck. With great precision the oarsmen abruptly changed the direction they were rowing, halting the ship in just a few strokes. Upon a subsequent command, they hauled their oars into the ship, preventing them being smashed by the disembarking legionaries.

Master Centurion Tyranus blew his whistle. Without further commands, Magnus stepped over the rail and leapt into the rolling waves. He kicked his legs out as soon as he hit the water, allowing himself to sink down to his bottom rather than risk injury to his ankles. He stood up with a loud splash, completely drenched and tasting the salt water on his lips. The water was cold, causing many a startled shout from plunging legionaries. Magnus hoisted his shield high out of the water and began to trek through the waist-high swells. Hundreds of legionaries were following him and the other centurions, rushing into the sea and forming into a column as they made their way towards the beach. There was little need for shouted orders from the centurions, options, or decani. The cohort was a precision machine, with each soldier knowing his place. They did not have far to go, for the tide was low and it was only about fifty meters from where they jumped to the beach. The sandbar was surprisingly firm, negating the annoying amount of sand each soldier kicked into his sandals as they jogged up the beach.

As they scrambled up towards the tall grasses at the edge of the beach, Master Centurion Tyranus blew his whistle. The aquilifer raised the legion's eagle standard high.

"Third Century on me!" Magnus shouted, raising his gladius and blowing his whistle three times.

As chaotic as their disembarking over the sides of the ships seemed, any observers on the ridge would have marvelled at the incredible precision with which thousands of legionaries storming up the beach formed into their large battle formation. The aquilifer marched at the very head, the eagle now draped over his shoulder. Directly behind him was the centurion primus pilus. His First Century of the First Cohort occupied the very centre. Magnus' Third Century fell in on their immediate right, the Fifth Century next to them, with the Second and Fourth Centuries on Tyranus' left. Each century advanced as its own entity of six ranks, with standard bearers marching just behind their centurions.

All along the coastline, hosts of imperial legionaries were disembarking from their respective transports; centurions reforming their men once they reached the beach. Four additional cohorts fell

44

in with the First, two on each side, with the remaining five cohorts forming a reserve battle line behind them. Auxilia infantrymen were establishing their formations well out to the flanks of the legion. Their light skirmishers were already making their way towards the far ridgeline. Only the cavalry still remained aboard ship. The task of getting horses off the transports was a slow and painstaking process, and they needed the landing point secured before they could disembark.

The beach soon gave way to tall grasses on firmer ground. The sun shone through white, puffy clouds, as a pleasant breeze blew in from the sea. The gusts caused the soaked legionaries to shiver, though they hoped the sun would warm them soon enough. Were they not all armed for battle, it would have been the perfect day for relaxation at the seaside. Given the utter silence, as well as the beauty of the landscape, one would never know they were on the shores of an entirely hostile land. There had been no resistance yet, but there was no mistaking this was an invasion.

As the legion continued its march, the footfalls of five thousand men sounded its cadence upon the earth. Auxilia infantry cohorts began to secure the ground just past the beach, while crewmen aboard the animal transport began the tedious task of getting the cavalry horses and pack animals off the ships. They erected a large crane which would lift each horse or mule in a sling under its belly, lowering it into the sea below, where a dozen handlers waited. The process was slow and ponderous. Several horses and a large number of pack mules panicked as they were lowered into the rolling surf. A number of men wound up with cracked ribs and various bruises from the unruly beasts.

At the top of the ridge Tyranus raised his hand and the cornicen blew a long note on his horn, signalling for the legion to halt. Another series of horn blasts alerted the cohort commanders, who converged on the eagle standard.

"We'll establish camp here," the master centurion ordered. He pointed towards a lone tree about a quarter mile away. "Post the eagle there. Have all surveyors begin laying out the camp perimeters."

"What about reconnaissance, sir?" Centurion Metellus of the Fifth Cohort asked.

"There's little we can do until the cavalry have their horses off the ships. Governor Scapula and General Paulinus should be coming ashore within the hour. While surveyors lay out the camp, dispatch half your men to provide security. Post pickets three hundred meters from camp. The rest can begin claiming each cohort's baggage. Entrenching tools should have been stored at the top of the cargo holds."

While legionaries of the First Cohort were exempt from fatigue details while in garrison, they still had to erect their own tents and entrench their section of the camp's defences while on campaign. Magnus walked over to what would be the northern boundary of the camp and scanned the horizon.

"Nothing," Tyranus said, as he joined him. "Not a gods-damned thing. One would think this whole region was entirely devoid of humanity."

"Oh, they're out there," the Nordic centurion replied, removing his helmet and scratching away at the still-damp mop of hair. "But with no knowledge of the region, we are running blind."

"Indus' Horse will be kept busy, no doubt about that. I almost wish the enemy had been waiting for us on the beach instead of making us go find him."

What neither of the centurions knew was that the ridge had not been entirely deserted. A lone rider lurked within one of the many groves of trees dotting the landscape. He'd watched the entire division disembark, doing his best to estimate the invaders' strength. He had to warn his chieftain and, more importantly, find Caratacus!

Something else neither Scapula nor any of his soldiers knew was just how close to Caratacus they had landed. After two days of hard riding, the panic-stricken messenger from the Deceangli rode into the camp at Halkyn Mountain. The Catuvellauni Prince had only just that morning received oaths of unflinching support from his allies in the war against Rome.

"Great Caratacus, Chief of the Catuvellauni, I bring grave news!" the man said, practically falling from his horse before dropping down onto one knee. It was quite telling that he prostrated himself before Caratacus rather than King Seisyll, who was overlord of both the Ordovices the Deceangli.

"Rise, my friend," Caratacus said, helping the man to his feet. "Now, what is this cause of distress among our friends on the northern shores?" Though his voice and demeanour remained calm, he knew the message to be grim. His fears were confirmed when the messenger spoke again.

"The Romans have landed. I saw their ships sailing past our shores, and they have a huge force encamped ten miles east of our capital at Kanovium."

This was distressing news. The bulwark of the Silures and Ordovices armies were several days away, seeking to ambush what they thought was the entire Roman invasion force near the River Sabrina. That a second imperial division of equal size had gone around the peninsula and landed behind them meant plans would have to change quickly.

"If they sailed right past Kanovium, they must not even know that it's there," Seisyll reasoned.

"They'll find it soon enough," Caratacus conjectured. "They have no knowledge of these lands, yet they will send their scouts out in every direction." He asked the messenger, "How many men do they have?"

"Ten thousand, at least. I saw one of their eagles and a slew of other standards."

King Orin spoke up, his voice filled with growing anger. "And with most of our warriors several days south of here, we have not the numbers to face them." He shook his head. "We should have launched an attack on their land division and dispersed them while they were on the march!"

While Caratacus appreciated the valour and tenacity of the Silures, he knew King Orin was prone to recklessness. "To do so would mean sending fifty thousand warriors deep into Roman lands. They would have ambushed us, as we intend to do to them."

"Besides, your warriors lack the discipline to remain organized long enough to take part in such a vast undertaking," Seisyll scoffed. Though allies they may have been, the old animosities between their kingdoms would not so easily die.

Caratacus took a few moments to contemplate this new threat. "Our enemy is clever, but he has also committed himself to serious

47

risk by dividing his forces. King Orin, I would ask that you return to your army and make ready to harry and delay the Roman army in the south. I will remain here with King Seisyll. We will draw this invasion force deep into the mountains southwest of here. Once they are lost and scattered, we can converge our forces to deal with the invaders coming up from the south."

The kings agreed. Orin, however, was beginning to feel pangs of animosity towards his blood-brother, who was now all but giving him orders. The messenger from Deceangli looked at Caratacus in horror. "But…what of us? What of our people? Who will save us?"

"Courage is your best defence this day," King Seisyll said, almost dismissively. The Deceangli were one of his protectorates; however, they would now have to take a stand themselves, earning the protecting the Ordovices had given them all these years.

Chapter V: Slaves of Fear

Roman Camp near Kimmel Bay
***

"Sir, we've located a large hillfort not ten miles from here," Commander Julianus from Indus' Horse reported. "We believe it could be the Deceangli capital."

"If they're that close, then they are already aware of our presence," Paulinus reasoned.

Julianus confirmed his assessment. "We saw large numbers of people fleeing the stronghold. They were mostly weighted down with whatever possessions they could carry. Others were leading livestock towards the southwest."

"Dispatch your cavalry and light auxilia in pursuit," Scapula ordered. "General Paulinus, detach six cohorts to envelop the stronghold. Two companies of archers will provide skirmishers. Unfortunately, we lack heavy siege engines, just four onagers and a dozen scorpions."

One of the harshest realities of launching an amphibious campaign was the limitations brought on by logistics. Even with most of the Britannic fleet ferrying them around the isle, there was only so much space aboard each ship. Siege engines were large and cumbersome, and from what little intelligence the Romans had about the Silures and Ordovices, the idea of building large, fortified strongholds was unknown to them. There was also the matter of transporting the heavy weapons, especially onagers, across such rugged terrain covered with near-impassable forests.

"That should be sufficient, sir," Julianus surmised. "The oppida is large but not well defended."

"Just don't get reckless, slaughtering those fleeing barbarians," Paulinus cautioned. "The Deceangli are under the protection of the Ordovices, so they could have friends waiting for us."

While the senior leaders made their tentative plan, word was sent to the six cohorts that would take part in the assault. The past few days had been spent fortifying their camp, while cleaning and oiling all of their weaponry and kit soaked during the landing. Punishment for allowing one's armour and weapons to become corroded by salt water residue was severe, often resulting in a flogging with the centurion's vine staff and a loss of pay. Having spent more than a day on their kit, each soldier was now ready to abandon the tedium of life in camp for a chance at battle and glory. There were many disgruntled mutterings, and more than a few profane curses, from the four cohorts designated to remain behind and guard the camp. Trumpets sounded as soldiers helped each other into their armour. Decani conducted quick inspections before reporting to their centurions and options.

For Centurion Magnus and his men, a benefit of being in the First Cohort was that they never got left behind on guard detail. With eight hundred elite soldiers in its ranks, the venerable First was always at the proverbial spear-point of any attack. Of course the chances of being killed or seriously injured also increased exponentially, but then, that was a risk they all willingly accepted.

Their tents were erected near the western entrance to the camp. As he buckled his sword baldric, Magnus watched scores of cavalrymen converge just beyond the ramparts and encircling trench. Commander Julianus was disseminating orders to his company commanders. Light auxilia skirmishers formed into groups of twenty to thirty, ready to accompany the horsemen in pursuit of the Deceangli fugitives. With a few last minute instructions from General Paulinus, Master Centurion Tyranus led the First Cohort out the hastily erected gate. They marched at the quick step, anxious for battle and the possibility of plunder. In addition to their weapons, General Paulinus ordered the men to bring two days' worth of rations, in case of an unexpected stay at the hillfort. The younger legionaries in the other cohorts were particularly eager and had to be reminded by their section leaders to calm themselves. Their objective was at least half-a-day's march from the camp, and they needed to save their strength for the coming battle.

While the Syrian archers formed a wide skirmish line approximately fifty meters forward of the main body, the aquilifer marched at the head of the legionaries, boldly carrying aloft the sacred imperial eagle. Legate Paulinus, the tribunes, and Master Centurion Tyranus rode near the aquilifer, escorted by twenty of the legion's indigenous horsemen. With only a narrow road, which was simply a well-worn dirt path used by farmers between settlements, most of the soldiers marched on either side in a pair of columns. The ground was mostly open grassland, perfect for farming. Scapula made mention of this to Paulinus.

"All the more reason for us to eventually conquer this land," the legate remarked. He then added an observance he'd made as a young man, while serving as chief tribune to one of the legions in Germania, "The true wealth of a land is not in its gold or jewels, but in how much of that land can be cultivated for agriculture."

"One cannot eat gold," Scapula added in concurrence. "Of course, I have heard rumours of there being a wealth of gold and other metals in the lands west of the Sabrina. The emperor will no doubt be pleased, should we acquire some of these riches for the empire. But the first thing we must do is destroy Caratacus and his resistance."

It was early afternoon when they came within earshot of the Deceangli capital. The sound of panicked screams echoed from beyond a large grove of trees just north of the path. Scapula rode forward as he saw a section of ten troopers from Indus' Horse riding towards them. They were arrayed in two files with nearly thirty oxen bearing baskets full of food stores, in addition to a score of sheep, between them.

"Commander Julianus' compliments, sir," a decurion said, saluting the governor. "We were ordered to take these 'mobile rations' back to camp."

"What of the people you took them from?" the governor asked.

"We slew any who attempted to resist and took probably a hundred prisoners. One of the infantry cohorts is sorting them out as we speak."

"Prisoners can be useful hostages," Paulinus noted.

Scapula shrugged dismissively. "Or at least they'll earn us a few denarii from the slave merchants." He nodded to the cavalry officer. "Good work, decurion."

"Sir!" The man saluted then led his section around the legionary columns.

Just then, a Syrian archer ran back towards the column, the remainder of their men having gone into the woods ahead.

"The barbarians have barricaded themselves in the oppida," he reported. "Just past the trees the ground opens up and about two hundred meters on, the path veers sharply to the right, leading directly up to the stronghold."

"We should see this for ourselves," Paulinus recommended. He turned to Tyranus. "Advance the legion to the wood line then stand by for further orders."

The legate was now taking control of the mission, something Scapula had come to accept. For though he was governor of the entire province of Britannia, he knew it best to allow his legates the freedom to utilize their troops as best they saw fit. A proud general like Suetonius Paulinus would become rather indignant, should the governor attempt to tell him how to command his legion.

While the legionaries continued their march, the governor, legate, and their escorts followed the archer into the woods. Due to the thickness of the undergrowth, they were obliged to dismount and make their way on foot. The far edge of the wood line was sparser of trees where locals had harvested much of the old forest. The capital itself encompassed a wide, short hill. It was surrounded by a thicket of long sharpened poles, not unlike the employment of palisade stakes by the legions. Numerous thatched huts and roundhouses, very similar to those seen in Germania, covered the sides of the hill. At the very top was a large structure towering over the others. A long building sloped upward, it was the local chief's longhouse.

"Seems straightforward enough," Scapula remarked. "Cut off any escape routes. Then we go knock on the door and see who is home."

Paulinus gave a malicious grin. "I'll tell the lads to be on their best behaviour for our hosts."

"First Cohort, battle formation!"

At the order from Tyranus, each century formed into six ranks, javelins resting over their shoulders, ready to unleash. From his position near the edge of the woods, Magnus could see several upturned wagons and carts piled in front of the entrance to the settlement. Warriors with bows and stabbing spears stood defiantly behind the defences. The rest of the legion's cohorts surrounded the hill. The Deceangli left only one way in or out of their high chief's stronghold, thus trapping themselves behind its wall of stakes.

While the legionaries waited for the order to attack, the handful of scorpions brought with them were deployed to either side of the road. The much larger onagers were being wheeled into position. Having a substantially greater range than the enemy's bowmen, they commenced unleashing their missiles without any threat of reprisal. A barbarian defender cried out when he was struck in the shoulder. The heavy bolt burst through flesh and muscle, splintering bone. Another man was hit in the stomach, doubling him over in horrifying pain as his guts were impaled. The remaining warriors hid low behind the barricades, the cries of their dying companions unnerving them.

"Use flaming shot and concentrate on the barricades," Paulinus ordered the catapult crews.

It took several minutes to fill the clay pots with oil and load them into the onagers' throwing arms. They were then ignited, and with a loud slap of the throwing arm, flung in a high arc towards the stronghold. One of the flaming projectiles smashed into the ground in front of the defences, two more sailed high and burst among the rooftops of the clustered huts. The fourth crashed into the barricades with a spray of fire, causing the enemy warriors to scramble away, where they were subjected to another barrage from the scorpions.

The onagers fired several more salvos, and though the bombardment of flaming missiles was indeed terrifying, they were not having their intended effect. Each would shatter upon impact and burn for a few moments, but the wood and thatch was simply too damp for the flames to take hold.

"Rains too damn much here," a staff tribune grumbled.

Paulinus nodded and then wordlessly drew his spatha. He raised the weapon high and brought it down in a sharp swing. The cornicen sounded the order to attack. With shouts of *"Advance!"* from the cohort commanders, several thousand legionaries stepped off towards the heights. They marched in close order, practically shield-to-shield, while scorpions continued to suppress the barbarians. Several more Deceangli killed or badly injured in the barrage. As the legionaries made their way up the hill, the scorpions were compelled to cease their onslaught. When the Romans were within fifty feet of the barricades the warriors rose up, unleashing a torrent of their own missiles; arrows, throwing darts, sling stones.

"Down!" Magnus shouted.

His men quickly dropped to one knee, hunkering low behind their shields. Those in the second to sixth ranks held their shields overhead, forming a protective shell around the entire century. The rest of the cohort was doing the same. All the while, a company of nearly a hundred Syrian archers raced forward. From behind the protection of the legionary testudos, they loosed a series of volleys at their adversaries.

Realizing their missiles were all but useless against the legionary shield wall, the Deceangli warriors turned their attention to the archers. Arrows, spears, and stones flew over the heads of the armoured soldiers, felling several of the Syrian auxiliaries.

"Charge!" the Norse centurion shouted, lunging to his feet.

With a loud battle cry, the host of legionaries swarmed the defences. The archers' diversion bought them only a few moments, yet moments were all they needed.

The battle front of the First Cohort was very wide. Even when formed into six ranks, each century's frontage was still twenty-six soldiers wide. Tyranus and his century stormed the barricades while Magnus and the rest of the cohort contended with the stakes and earthworks. The panicked warriors haphazardly flung what missiles they had at the charging wall of legionaries before retreating into the town. The soldiers' armour offered excellent protection, yet one unlucky man took a throwing spear through the neck. His shield and pilum fell from his hands as he tumbled to the earth, his life's blood gushing from the hideous wound. Another had a sling stone deflect off the cheek guard of his helmet, breaking the hinges that held it in place. His comrade next to him was not as fortunate. Another barbarian slinger found his mark, the stone smashing into the Roman's face. The legionary screamed, hands over his face, falling to his knees in agony.

The spikes that jutted from the defences were very large, with one row thrust straight out and the second protruding upwards at an angle. The Deceangli used larger logs for their stakes to make them appear more menacing, yet they proved easier to climb over. Magnus' legionaries flung their javelins towards any enemy warriors they spotted, before beginning the awkward climb over the ramparts. Many dropped their shields, to better pull themselves up over the spikes, having their friends pass the shields up to them once they reached the top.

Making certain he was one of the first over the ramparts, Magnus now stood atop the earthworks and surveyed the confusion

54

within the settlement. Enemy fighters came from every direction, wielding mostly spears and wooden shields. A few carried hand axes or large, two-handed clubs. Only a few wielded swords, and these men also wore mail armour with bronze helmets. The wealthiest and most powerful men in this land were still less equipped than even the humblest legionary. One of these men shouted some orders and pointed towards the centurion with his longsword. Magnus reached back over the palisades to retrieve his shield, then quickly grabbed one of his legionaries by the hand and helped him over. He hefted his shield and turned to face the coming assault.

A warrior swung his hand axe towards Magnus' shin. The centurion quickly dropping his shield to deflect the blow. He kicked the man hard in the face with his hobnailed sandals, splitting open his forehead. The centurion leapt from the earthworks, slamming the bottom edge of his shield into the dazed warrior's face.

A sharp pain shot through the Norseman's leg, an incessant reminder of his old injury. His other knee buckled slightly. With his blood rushing through his veins, he scarcely noticed.

He was soon joined by growing numbers of his legionaries, forming into battle lines as more Deceangli fighters rushed into the fray. The huts and other structures within the settlement were built practically on top of each other, making for very narrow roads. The alleyways between buildings were so contracted that a single man could scarcely navigate through them. Warriors battered the shield wall with spears and axes, while legionaries punched away with their shields, seeking openings for thrusts of their gladii. The rear ranks of the cohort were now scrambling over the ramparts, and most of these men still carried their pila. From their high point on the earthworks, they flung their heavy javelins over the heads of their mates. A score of Deceangli warriors fell dead or badly wounded in the storm. The courage of the survivors momentarily wavered, giving Magnus and his soldiers the momentum needed to completely break them. Warriors who hesitated paid the price, as legionary blades plunged into their guts. Others had their arms or legs hacked when the Romans surged forward. The centurion himself thrust his gladius deep into the neck of one assailant, ripping the weapon free in a torrent of splattering blood. The will of the remaining fighters broke, and they fled for what they hoped would be sanctuary within the town.

Magnus led his century towards the barricades where, surprisingly, Master Centurion Tyranus' century was being hard-pressed to break through. The Deceangli had massed the largest portion of their warriors here, along with many of their skirmishers.

"Reform!" the Norseman shouted, holding his bloodied gladius high. Streams of dark crimson ran from the pommel of his weapon down his scarred, muscular forearm.

The open square near the barricade was filled with enemy warriors who were inexplicably oblivious to the growing mass of imperial soldiers about to flank them. Some of Magnus' legionaries managed to form into three ranks of twenty men. The rest of the century, along with Optio Caelius, was unable to advance any further. These men proceeded to kick down the walls of several mud huts, while others found windows to breach on wooden structures.

"Advance!"

The legionaries marched in step, their centurion having placed himself in the very centre. When they were but twenty feet away Magnus howled in fury, sprinting the remaining distance and smashing into a barbarian fighter with all his weight behind his shield. Only a handful of the Deceangli noticed them in time to turn and face this renewed threat. Shield bosses and blows from the bottom edges of Roman shields sent a number of their adversaries sprawling onto the ground. Several more were slain by lightning quick thrusts of legionary gladii.

As Tyranus and his century smashed their way through and over the barricade, toppling a pair of upturned oxcarts, the booming sound of a war horn came from near the high chief's great hall. Its meaning became immediately apparent. Warriors began to throw down their weapons and raise their hands in surrender. A couple were killed by overzealous legionaries, who were quickly berated by their officers.

"Hold fast, lads!" Tyranus bellowed as he clambered over a large broken wagon.

Most of the Deceangli warriors stood with their heads bowed in defeat. Others tried to tend to their badly wounded friends, who lay sprawled about the battleground.

"Do any of you speak Latin?" the master centurion asked, drawing confused stares. He shook his head in irritation and called over his shoulder, *"Send our interpreter forward…and inform General Paulinus that we've taken the town!"*

A few minutes of awkward silence followed, with neither warrior nor legionary knowing exactly what they should do. The other cohorts from the Twentieth Legion had breached the defences with a number of troops surrounding the chief's hall. Paulinus soon appeared at the barricade. With him was Landon, the Brigantes interpreter.

"Well done," the legate said approvingly. "Tyranus, take twenty of your men and come with me. The rest of you, start binding and sorting these prisoners."

"Yes, sir," the primus pilus nodded.

"Centurion Magnus, take charge of the cohort."

Magnus nodded and ordered his men to lead their defeated foes out of the town onto the open plain below. As they guided the prisoners down the slope, he was joined by Centurion Furius.

He noticed Magnus was walking with a pronounced limp. "Almost sent you to Valhalla, didn't they?"

Magnus smiled and shook his head. "No, just the past injuries of an old man." He winked as he looked at a rather nasty gash on Furius' cheek. "That's the worst shaving cut I've ever seen."

His fellow centurion primus ordo sighed and gently touched the still-bleeding wound with his fingertips. "Twenty-two years in the ranks without any visible scars and now this. It's my own damned fault. I didn't tie the chin cords on my helmet tight enough, and the cheek guards were flapping about. And it would seem I was slower with my shield than the cohort's 'old man'."

The two shared a laugh as their legionaries began to sort the prisoners. Their hands were bound behind their backs, and each man was tied to the warrior behind him. Their dead and maimed were left where they fell. For the Romans, it had not been a costless victory. Seven legionaries and four auxilia archers had been killed, with another forty men wounded between them. Half of these injured soldiers would likely be fit to return to duty in a few days; the rest would have to be evacuated to a hospital in Roman territory. Scapula's intent was to have the imperial navy transport enemy prisoners and Roman wounded back to Camulodunum, when they arrived with the army's next resupply.

The chief of Deceangli was an older warrior named Elisedd. He was surrounded by a score of legionaries who stood close with their weapons drawn. He wore a long leather frock covered in small, rectangular bronze plates, belted in the middle. A sword baldric hung over his right shoulder. His weapon, a magnificent two-handed longsword, had been confiscated and was being held by a decanus. Standing beside him, her expression one of defiance, was his wife, Runa. She kept her plaid cloak held close around her shoulders, her auburn hair pulled back tight against her scalp.

The chief's brow was sweaty, his complexion red from exertion. For him, the battle had not lasted long. From his vantage point atop the hill, his stronghold swarming with imperial soldiers, he knew all was lost. He bowed to the General Paulinus as the decanus handed the chief's sword to the legate.

"Yr wyf yn ostyngedig yn cynnig fy ildio," Elisedd said, in a language that Paulinus could not even begin to comprehend. *"Pa tynged yn aros fy mhobl?"*

"He says he humbly offers his surrender," Landon translated, speaking slowly, as he struggled to understand all the chief was saying, "I believe he's asking what fate awaits his people."

"He and his warriors are to be taken to Governor Scapula who will decide the ultimate fate of the Deceangli."

Landon translated the legate's words causing Elisedd to grimace. He had little to no faith in the honour of the imperial governor, yet sadly, he knew he was powerless. The Romans had been too numerous for his warriors to make a viable stand. The Deceangli were mostly fishermen and farmers, bullied into subjugation by the far more numerous and warlike Ordovices with the promise of 'protection'. And with the Ordovices nowhere to be found, their protectorates were left to the mercy of their enemies.

Chapter VI: Finding the Enemy

Roman Camp near Kimmel Bay
19 June 48 A.D.
***

Paulinus ordered all food stores from the oppida to be taken back to camp. The stronghold was then put to the torch. It took some time for the damp timbers to ignite, and the thick columns of black smoke could be seen for twenty miles. Governor Scapula had ridden back to the Roman camp once he saw the stronghold was taken by his soldiers. His principia tent served as a tribunal in which he would meet the defeated Deceangli chieftain.

In all, nearly three thousand prisoners were taken. Most of those captured at the stronghold were warriors. The fighting men had sent their women and children away, hoping they might escape. The sight of many of their families penned up in the crude stockades told a grim tale. The captured warriors could also assume many of their loved ones had been killed. They were kept separate from the women and children, and there was no way for anyone to know who was imprisoned, dead, or managed to escape.

Scapula made certain his armour was polished, and he draped his finest deep red cloak over his left shoulder. He sat upon a three-foot dais, just large enough for his camp chair. To his right sat a five-foot pillar with a bust of Emperor Claudius atop, to his left the eagle of the Twentieth Legion and the standards of Indus Horse and the other auxilia regiments. General Paulinus, Commander Julianus, the tribunes, First Cohort centurions, and auxilia regimental commanders stood on either side of the dais.

Elisedd and Runa and ten of their nobles were escorted into the principia. Their hands were chained in front of them. Elisedd carried his sword, resting flat on the palms of his hands. Landon walked in front of the escorting legionaries. Once they reached the dais, the Brigantes interpreter relayed the orders he had been given earlier. Elisedd was to kneel before Scapula and plant his sword point into the earth. It was terribly degrading for the proud war chief; however, he knew the option was to watch every last one of his captured warriors be crucified. The women and children would likely be sold into slavery, regardless of what their chief did. The Romans had promised to spare Runa, however, should her husband offer total submission to the empire.

With overwhelming feelings of both humiliation and stalwart determination, Elisedd girded his dignity and knelt in front of the dais. He thrust the sword, passed down for generations, into the earth. He fought back tears as his grip lingered on the worn handle, for what he knew to be the last time. The ancient blade was now a prize of Caesar.

The Deceangli chief took a slow breath in and exhaled quietly, composing himself. Finally he spoke, *"Trwy waed fy hynafiaid, yr wyf yn tyngu ar fy mywyd sydd byth eto bydd fy mhobl yn gwneud rhyfel yn erbyn Rhufain."*

Landon remained stoic, though he was moved by the beaten warrior's words. He translated, *"By the blood of my ancestors, I swear on my life that never again will my people make war against Rome."*

And though Elisedd had not asked this directly, the Brigantes man decided to ask on his behalf, "What is to become of their people?"

"War against Rome requires a measure of retribution," Scapula explained, speaking slowly so Landon could translate. "You and your wife will be taken to Rome, where you may plead your case before the emperor. He will decide the ultimate fate of Deceangli. Your warriors, as well as their women and children, will remain hostages of Rome to ensure the good faith of your people. Understand, any further acts of violence against the empire and their lives will become forfeit."

Frustrated that their fate remained undecided, Elisedd simply nodded as he stood. Scapula signalled to the legionaries surrounding the couple, who escorted them from the principia.

"Hostages?" Paulinus asked. "Between the warriors and the families the auxilia captured, we have over four thousand prisoners. Even with the food stores we took from their stronghold, they will starve within two weeks."

"By which time our resupply ships will have arrived," Scapula explained. "I directed Admiral Stoppello to bring additional rations, as well as any equipment we were unable to transport during the initial landing. He can take these...*hostages*... off our hands then."

"You don't intend to ever release them," the legate said knowingly. "You're going to hand them over to the slave traders."

"And what would you do, General Paulinus, were you Governor of Britannia? Would you commit the resources to feed and house several thousand prisoners from a tribe that matters little in this war? Had we crushed the Silures and Ordovices first, the Deceangli would have capitulated without a fight. Unlucky that their homeland happened to be right in our invasion path, isn't it?"

Paulinus bit the inside of his cheek. While their deceit was a bit troubling, he knew Scapula was right. The legate was coming to understand, should he ever wish to rise above his posting of legion commander and govern an imperial province, he would have to think beyond just winning battles. While Ostorius Scapula was scarcely an adequate military strategist, and having committed several serious diplomatic blunders early in his term as governor, he was proving to be a viable teacher to the legate when it came to dealing with newly-conquered peoples and unruly provincials. On the furthest frontiers of the empire, there was little room for clemency. For many of these people, ruthless brutality was the only form of persuasion they understood.

While Governor Scapula determined the interim fate of the Deceangli, Centurion Metellus Artorius led the Fifth Cohort, supported by two companies from Indus' Horse, in a massed reconnaissance to the southwest. It was the direction taken by most of the fleeing Deceangli, and Scapula intended to use them to locate the barbarians' main army. His intent was to gather as much intelligence as possible before linking up with General Paetus' division.

Most of the actual reconnaissance was done by the cavalry; Metellus and his legionaries were simply there for support, should the horsemen run into a larger force than they could contend with. As the senior officer present, Metellus ordered the cavalry commanders to make certain they kept his legionaries in view at all times. While traversing open terrain, this meant the auxilia troopers could keep one hill or ridgeline away. Crossing the innumerable forests, the cavalry waited until the infantry was within thirty meters or less before proceeding.

Approximately four miles into their trek, they came upon a dirt trail that led in a westerly direction. The ground was saturated from the recent rains, which made tracking their quarry much easier.

"There are no recent tracks along this stretch of road, sir," a trooper reported.

"Which means they did not come this way," Metellus noted.

The trooper nodded and then continued, "We sent two sections to see where this leads. We haven't seen much in the way of farmlands; however, we believe these people to be mostly sheepherders. There are plenty of signs of grazing, not to mention copious amounts of sheep shit. Any villages will be small and scattered about these grassy hills."

The centurion sent the trooper back to his company. He continued on with his legionaries two more miles, where they came upon a small brook. "We'll hold here until the scouts return," he directed his men.

His centuries formed into a defensive hollow square and soldiers were sent to fill water bladders in the stream.

"I've counted our pace, and we've gone about six miles," one of the centurions stated.

"We'll go another four before turning back," the pilus prior replied.

Most of the cavalrymen had also halted at the stream to water their horses and sate their own thirsts. Sections of troopers were dispatched in each direction to find some sign of the fugitives. The sun was now directly overhead, and though it shone brightly, dark clouds loomed in the west. A cool gust of wind blew over the cohort, warning of the gods' intentions.

"Just when we got our sodden clothes dried out," a legionary complained.

"And I thought the weather was wet and unpredictable on the rest of this isle," another added. "It's as if the gods are fucking with us. Give us the sun one minute, and then piss on us the next."

"Too bad Jupiter's piss is anything but warm," the first soldier added.

While legionaries carped about the constant and volatile changes to the region's weather, the sound of galloping horses alerted Metellus and his centurions to the return of the reconnaissance detachment. A cavalry centurion rode out to meet his troopers, who briefed him quickly before reporting to Metellus.

"We found a settlement about six miles to the west," the cavalry section leader said, dismounting his horse. He used a stick to draw a crude map in the mud. "This stream meets with the road about a mile before the village. There wasn't much there, mostly round huts and a few animal pens."

"Any idea where they went?" a centurion asked.

"There were numerous sets of tracks, both human and animal, headed southwest. I rode to the nearest hilltop and got a good look in that direction, right where those storm clouds are coming from."

"So at least they're getting pissed on before us," a centurion remarked with bitter humour.

"It's extremely mountainous that way," the trooper continued. "From what we've seen, most of this region is rolling hills and grasslands, with a number of tree groves and thick forests. But if you keep going west or southwest, the terrain becomes extremely rough and extremely rocky."

With this fresh bit of knowledge, Metellus decided to confer with his centurions before proceeding further. The cavalry scouts had confirmed the route the refugees were taking. Was there really any point in his small taskforce advancing further? They likely had as much actionable intelligence as they were going to attain this day. It would be best to report their findings to General Paulinus as soon as possible. The discussion was brief, and with the storm clouds advancing from the southwest, the entire cohort was anxious to return to camp. Metellus was about to inform the lead centurion to screen their march back, when they heard shouting from where several men were watering their horses.

"Oi! Stop right there, you filthy bastard!"

There was a loud crashing in one of the thickets, and a tall, slender man was seen sprinting away from the contingent. Clad in only a loincloth and sandals, his skin was painted with a series of strange blue markings.

"Get that son of a whore!" a cavalry section leader shouted.

"Alive!" Metellus bellowed after the troopers. "Bring that man to me alive!"

"Think it's a scout?" one of his centurions asked.

"If so, he's a sloppy one," the pilus prior grunted. "We'll find out who he is soon enough." He addressed his men. *"Fifth Cohort, fall in!* It's only six miles back to camp. Let's see if we can make it back before the storm gods of this land wash us away."

It took only minutes for a pair of troopers to track down their prey. He made no attempt to defend himself, his only weapon being a small curved sword. Riding at full speed, a mounted lancer smashed him in the back of the head with the butt of his spear. The concussed man's hands were bound behind his back, and he was gruffly dragged back to Centurion Metellus.

"Rwy'n dod o Caratacus!" the prisoner screamed over and over, his eyes wide and mouth slobbering in rage.

He added a slew of other biting shouts that the Romans assumed were either threats or insults. Metellus surmised that the man was not of the Deceangli, for none of their warriors had been painted blue. Whoever he was, it was unlikely that he expected to find imperial soldiers in this area, or he would have been more cautious.

"A messenger probably," a centurion surmised. "Bad spot of luck that in this whole damned region he happened to run right into us."

"Perhaps the local gods are fucking with them as well," another remarked. "Either that or ours are simply stronger than theirs."

Metellus and the barbarian continued to glare at each other.

The pilus prior then said, "Whatever he is, he has information we want. Let's get him back to General Paulinus and hope our interpreter can speak his frightful tongue."

The constant invoking of the name 'Caratacus' caught the centurion's attention; indeed, it was the only word any of the Romans understood. Scapula and Paulinus assumed it was the Catuvellauni prince who had united the mountain peoples, and it seemed their assumptions were about to be proven correct.

With the wind whipping their cloaks about, the soldiers of the Fifth Cohort marched at a quick pace, almost jogging. The enemy messenger's hands were bound to a cavalryman's horse. He was quick on his feet, though a trooper continued to prod him with his lance the entire trek back. An hour into their march, the skies blackened, and the heavens opened with an unholy torrent.

"Son of a whore!" a legionary grumbled.

The Romans had built their camp on a ridge overlooking the sea. The ground was much sandier than the hardened clay and soil further inland, proving fortuitous, for the drainage offered by the sloping, porous ground saved the camp from flooding. It rained often in other parts of Britannia, but nothing prepared them for the downpour they were now subjected to. Legionaries on sentry duty were soon drenched, despite having their large cloaks wrapped around them. The echoing of rain off their helmets was so loud, they could only communicate by shouting.

During this deluge, the Fifth Cohort and the reconnaissance cavalry returned. Legionaries were trying to move with haste, yet the tall grasses flattened by the rains made the ground slippery. A number of soldiers lost their footing and fell onto their backsides, much to the amusement of their mates. Once inside the large compound, Metellus tasked a squad from his own century to accompany him and their prisoner to the principia. The rest of his men were dismissed. Orders were shouted over the downpour by their respective centurions, directing them to clean and polish their armour and kit and be ready for full inspection the next day. For the soldiers in the ranks, they were only too glad to get out of the torrent, and further relieved that they were exempt from guard detail.

The prisoner had since ceased in his berating of the soldiers. His eyes were wide in awe at the formidable sight of the Roman encampment. He had never seen so many armoured fighters in his life.

At the principia, a pair of legionaries huddled beneath their cloaks outside the entrance. They came to attention and saluted the centurion, their gazes fixed on the strange barbarian. The prisoner's blue body paint had started to wash away. The designs, meant to offer protection, were smeared across his skin, as if his gods were mocking him for his carelessness.

Inside, Governor Scapula and General Paulinus gathered around a large parchment, where the legion's chief cartographer attempted to map out the terrain they had explored thus far. The pummelling rains echoed off the high tent roof, making it difficult to converse.

"Ah, Centurion Metellus," Paulinus said. "And what have you brought us?"

"Either a scout or a messenger, sir," Metellus replied. "To be honest, I'm not sure which. None of our men speak his tongue, and my guess is he doesn't know Latin or Greek. But we did catch one name he kept saying over and over again...Caratacus."

"I'll be damned," Scapula said, watching the man twitch at the mention of Caratacus' name. "So it is him we are pursuing after all."

"Yes, sir. The interrogators will learn what he knows soon enough."

"Indeed they will." He turned to Landon, who stood in the shadows. He swallowed hard, knowing this next tasking would not be pleasant. The governor addressed him and one of his scribes. "You will take this...man...to the interrogation detachment. Write down everything he tells you."

The men nodded and followed Metellus' legionaries back out into the storm. The pilus prior was directed to return as soon as he had his supper. The legion's torture detachment was close by, and it was fortunate for all that the pounding rains would drown out the cries of their victim.

With the torrential storm still hammering the encampment, the skies darkened well before nightfall. Lamps were lit within the principia. All cohort commanders, centurion primus ordo, and staff tribunes joined the commanding legate and governor. Between screams of agony and curses at the Romans, the prisoner told them he was a messenger from Caratacus, sent to gather warriors from the Deceangli for the coming battle against the Roman army.

"So, Caratacus doesn't even know we are here," Scapula conjectured.

"Sir, this intelligence is at least a week old," Paulinus countered. "I would say it is very likely Caratacus is now aware of our presence. Some of the refugees will have sought out his army rather than fleeing for the mountains. And besides, anyone within twenty miles would have seen the billowing columns of smoke where we torched the Deceangli stronghold."

The governor turned to Julianus. "Is there any way you could get a message to General Paetus?"

The cavalry officer shook his head. "I doubt it. We don't know the layout of this land, and we must assume the enemy has every passable road between here and Roman territory swarming with fighters. We're not even sure where Paetus is. Even if I took my entire regiment, the chances of reaching him without being overtaken by Caratacus is extremely risky."

"Then perhaps aggression will be our best course of action," the governor reasoned. "We now know where Caratacus is, thanks to our new 'friend'. Our division numbers ten thousand men, which should be sufficient to take the fight to them."

"I would not recommend that, sir," Centurion Magnus spoke up.

All eyes turned to the Norseman.

"We fought against the Silures during the invasion. Of all the tribes who dared oppose us, they were the most difficult to defeat. They are better equipped than most 'barbarians' and highly skilled in battle. They may not be professional soldiers, but they are the closest to it of any tribe in Britannia. Between them and the Ordovices, they likely outnumber us substantially."

"What would you recommend, centurion?" Paulinus asked.

Magnus walked over and ran his finger in a line down the map, from their encampment to the stream Metellus' cohort had discovered. "This area here is all open ground, ideal for rapid movement. The terrain to the south is extremely rugged, making difficult for a large army to manoeuvre. If we place ourselves here, we cut Caratacus off from his food supplies."

"The Deceangli were providing the enemy with warriors and, more importantly, rations," Master Centurion Tyranus added. "They have no real concept of supply lines or logistics. Hence why their campaign seasons are so short. Those abandoned sheep villages the Fifth Cohort discovered were probably supplying food and wool to Caratacus."

"True, but we only found a couple of them," Metellus spoke up. "There could be any number out there that are not abandoned."

"No matter," Tyranus remarked. "If we create a blockade between Caratacus and the Deceangli lands, their army will be compelled to disperse, risk starving, or face us in battle."

Paulinus concurred. "With suitable defences, fighting on ground of our choosing, we can negate their superior numbers."

However strategically sound their plan may have been, Scapula's face betrayed his lingering doubts. He frowned and slowly shook his head. "We risk spreading ourselves thin," he said. "I would rather take a bold chance and attack Caratacus head-on. If he knows where General Paetus' division is and knows we're here, he will feel caught between our armies. His warriors may panic."

"Respectfully, sir, if you think the Silures will panic, you underestimate them," Magnus stated. "And given that they never defeated the Ordovices, who I may add we've never faced in battle, I suspect their valour is at least their equal."

"Halkyn Mountain is thirty miles from here, maybe more," Commander Julianus added. He glanced up at the ceiling of the principia tent, where incessant torrents of rain still echoed. "One can bet the ground between here and there has been churned into a bog. My cavalry will be forced to advance at a crawl."

"It'll take two to three days to reach the mountain," Paulinus remarked. "We could use that time to establish our blockade, with suitable defence works…"

"Those are your orders," the governor interrupted, not bothering to hide his growing irritation. "While I appreciate your collective skill and experience, I find it unbecoming that imperial soldiers are hesitant to take the fight to the enemy. We depart at sunrise, the rains be damned. *Dismissed.*"

Chapter VII: A Sacrifice of Blood

Halkyn Mountain, Four Miles West of the River Dubr Duiu
22 June 48 A.D.

Halkyn Mountain

Scapula ordered two auxilia infantry cohorts to remain at the main camp to guard the wounded, along with the numerous prisoners. Admiral Stoppello was expected to return within the next two weeks, depending on the weather and conditions at sea. At General Paulinus' recommendation, the onagers had been left behind, as the heavy wagons sank up to the axles in the mud. Much of the baggage, including the large principia tents, were also left at camp.

The trek to Halkyn Mountain took three days, just as General Paulinus had feared. The army crossed a seemingly endless number of rivers and creeks, which slowed their pace considerably, especially with pack animals. The rains had mercifully ceased, though the skies remained grey with dense clouds. Every step of the way was a slog through mud and slippery grass. Two companies from Indus' Horse provided reconnaissance. As Julianus predicted, their pace was scarcely better than that of the encumbered infantrymen. It was now late morning on the third day. Every soldier in the column was concerned about when the rains would come again, when a trooper from the vanguard rode back to Governor Scapula and General Paulinus.

"The barbarians have all hoofed it, sir," the messenger reported.

Scapula scowled. "How long ago?"

"No way of knowing. The entire mountain, along with much of the surrounding lowlands, are a trampled mess. Their army was huge."

Scapula halted the column and rode ahead with Paulinus, Tyranus, the staff tribunes, and First Cohort centurions. The ground in and around Halkyn was churned up by thousands of feet. There was also the unmistakable stench of numerous uncovered cesspits, as well as rotted sheep and other animal carcasses from the barbarians' meals. The senior officers met with the centurion in command of the advance guard, who sat astride his horse at the very top of the hill.

"We don't know when they left, sir, but we do know where they've gone," he reported.

"The lone benefit of the mud left by the rains," Paulinus observed.

"Very true, sir. The vast majority of their tracks are headed due west. Since we saw no sign of them yesterday or the day before, they must have left once they knew we were in the region, and we simply missed them."

"Meaning they are likely a week's trek from here," Scapula grunted.

While he shared in the governor's frustrations, General Paulinus' attention was not on Caratacus' army. "What of those who did not head west?" he asked the centurion.

"There are a large number of tracks—again, hard to say just how many—that are headed north."

"But there is nothing in that direction except the sea and the River Dubr Duiu," Scapula noted. "And if they cross the river, they will be in Roman territory."

Paulinus closed his eyes and tilted his head back in realization. "A raiding party," he said quietly. He supressed the urge to vent his frustrations, knowing they had lost a great opportunity to engage Caratacus in a decisive engagement. Adding to his chagrin, the enemy tracks showed they would have run right into Centurion Magnus' proposed blockade. Even worse now, the legate feared for their camp. The forces that headed north were likely not headed towards Roman territory, but the main camp near the sea. The prisoners and wounded, along with the two cohorts of auxilia infantry guarding them, were now in danger.

For the cohorts left at the camp, boredom seemed to be their greatest adversary. Though the legionaries and other auxilia cohorts had taken their palisade stakes with them, the earthworks had been left in place pending their return. Those left behind created a smaller set of defences within, enclosing the prisoner stockades, as well as their own tents. The food stores captured from the Deceangli were taken to this inner encampment to feed the soldiers and prisoners.

There was little to be done, other than digging a pair of long trenches, to accommodate the bodily waste of the prisoners. Three thousand warriors were crammed together into a single enclosure, with a thousand women and children in another nearby. A wretched stench blew over the camp from each, and flies began to swarm the sewage trenches.

Scapula was aware of the problem of dealing with the human waste. He'd ordered the commanding centurion to move the stockades every two to three days, burying the sewage trenches each time. It would be a hateful task for the auxilia troopers; one that compounded the frustration they felt at being left behind.

Only Chief Elisedd and his consort, Runa, were granted any measure of dignity. They were kept behind a wooden stockade, where they still had a measure of privacy. Their hands were left unbound and, per Governor Scapula's orders, they were fed and treated with much greater respect than their enslaved people.

"I hope the fleet gets here soon," a trooper on guard duty at the stockade said, his long scarf covering his face. "These filthy barbarians stink even worse than when we captured them."

"Our esteemed governor should have let us slaughter the men, have our way with the women, and be done with them," one of his companions complained. "If the fleet takes too long to pick this lot up, they'll all be dead from disease."

"And taking us with them, once their filthy pestilence spreads," another added, a rag tied around his nose and mouth. "Besides, it's not like he'll be sharing what coin he may get from the slave traders with us."

It was a bit of irony for an auxilia soldier to refer to the prisoners as 'barbarians'. Most of these infantrymen came from humble villages in Gaul, Belgica, and Germania. Their native homes were not unlike the Deceangli settlements they had sacked. Yet so anxious were they to prove themselves as Romans, some became overtly disdainful towards other indigenous peoples.

Unbeknownst to the Roman auxiliaries, their troubles would soon involve more than disposing of prisoners' shit. King Seisyll and four thousand of his best warriors lay in wait behind a series of rolling hills east of the camp.

Accompanying the king was the high druid, a tall man with white hair and long beard named Tathal. Whatever rivalries still existed between the various kingdoms in the far reaches of western Britannia, all still looked to the gods to guide them. In many ways, the druids held far greater sway over the common people than any of the kings.

"I want the traitors alive," Tathal hissed, his eyes filled with rage. "The gods demand Elisedd pay for his blasphemy."

While Seisyll was happy to exact revenge against his former client war chief, he understood this raid was as much about upsetting Roman morale as it was about appeasing the gods. Aeron, the god of battle, would undoubtedly be pleased with the Ordovices. On this day the king wore his ring mail armour, a skull cap helmet, and bronze bracers on his forearms. His dark-coloured tartan cloak was draped over both shoulders, pinned in place with a large copper torque on the left shoulder.

"As we suspected," Seisyll said to his warrior captains, who laid in the tall grass next to their king, watching their enemy's camp, "the Romans are off chasing shadows."

"We outnumber the men they left," one of his captains observed. "But they still possess strong defences."

The king sneered maliciously. "We are not here to beat the Romans, only to claim our prize…which they have so carelessly left undefended."

The timing was as catastrophic for the Roman auxilia as it was fortuitous to the Ordovices. Their commanding centurion had ordered them to break down and move the warriors' stockade, a task which took a hundred men to perform. Four centuries of infantrymen surrounded the Deceangli fighting men, brandishing their spears. The rest of the cohort stood by with their entrenching tools, ready to fill in the putrid trenches. This left the remaining cohort of eight hundred men to defend the entire camp.

The sound of an unfamiliar war horn sent chills up the collective spine of every auxilia solider. This was followed by a lone battle cry in a language none of them understood. Their eyes grew wide, the faces of their prisoners breaking into expressions of hope, as several thousand enemy warriors appeared from behind a ridgeline less than a quarter mile east of the camp. Centurions and section leaders shouted orders for their troopers to make ready to face the coming onslaught.

With the stockade temporarily dismantled, the prisoners still required guarding. The commander of the second cohort directed all but two hundred of his men to follow him to the defences. His last orders to those remaining would serve as an ominous warning to the Deceangli, provided any of them understood Latin. "Kill any of these bastards that try to resist!" With a touch of morbid initiative, a decanus and two troopers stabbed several random prisoners, eliciting shouts of rage and horror from the rest. Since the warriors were still bond together in a series of long rows, the dead weight of any corpses would act as anchors, should they try to escape.

With few missile weapons on either side, there was little the auxiliaries could do except man the ramparts and wait for their assailants to navigate the obstacle-laden entrenchments and palisade stakes. Momentum was lost for the Ordovices, for the six-foot trench was filled with spikes, snares, and other impediments. One warrior shrieked as he stepped directly onto a hidden spike. Others found themselves tripped up, sometimes falling onto stakes and caltrops. The sandy ground was difficult for the attackers to gain purchase on as they pulled themselves up the other side. Many thrust their spears into the slope, using them for leverage. Others used the rows of palisade stakes for hand-holds. The first brave souls onto the earthworks paid dearly for their audacity. One took a spear thrust to the chest. Another into his eye socket, giving an unholy shriek as blood spurted forth, leaving him thrashing on the ground, begging for death. A third was stabbed in the groin as he leapt onto the ramparts.

The Roman auxiliaries had formed a long battle line of three ranks. Their formation was looser than that of legionaries, keeping several feet between each other. And while they were often regarded as second-rate fighters, not to mention more expendable, they were still professional soldiers with far superior training and armament than their foes. As more warriors scaled over the earthworks, the weight of the Ordovices assault drove into their thin line, with several auxilia troopers being cut down as they were driven back into the camp. The assailants outnumbered the imperial soldiers almost three-to-one, yet they failed to press their advantage. Those who tried to break the Roman lines often fell victim to the overlapping walls of spears.

A series of individual brawls broke out along the line, and despite the protection offered by both their discipline and armour, the auxiliaries were still suffering casualties. Men on both sides could expect no mercy, and yet, because their enemies failed to launch the full weight of their horde against them, the Romans were getting the better of the exchange. With the constant crashing of spears against shields, none of the auxilia officers realized that they were simply being distracted from their adversaries' actual goal.

The attack on the prisoner stockade came from the west without war horns or battle cries. It was only when a nervous infantryman spied movement near the far embankments of the outer camp that he sounded the alarm. As the Roman officers shouted orders for their men to form battle lines, they were swarmed by nearly a thousand enemy assailants. A hundred more rushed towards the smaller, lone stockade. These men cared nothing for the Deceangli women and children, nor their cowardly warriors who had surrendered ignominiously to the Romans.

As the axes of Ordovices warriors hacked down the gate of the stockade, Elisedd thought he was being rescued by this old allies

74

and protectors. The fierce anger in the eyes of his 'saviours' soon told him otherwise. Before the war chief could say a word, a spear butt was slammed into his forehead, knocking him unconscious. His wife screamed but was smashed across the face by another warrior's fist. The two were then carried from the stockade, surrounded by a score of Ordovices warriors. As they passed the ongoing melee with the Roman auxilia, piteous cries came from the prisoners.

"Please, take us with you!"

"Our friends, do not abandon us!"

Fury overcoming them, several warriors began attacking their former allies. Twenty Deceangli prisoners were killed, with at least twice as many badly mauled before the enraged Ordovices heeded the calls of their leaders to desist.

At the eastern ramparts, the attacking warriors heard the high-pitched sound of the war horn ordering their retreat. This proved problematic for those directly engaging the Roman auxilia. As Ordovices fighters climbed over the palisade stakes and tumbled back into the trench below, the imperial troopers surged forward, intent on slaying as many as possible. Their overzealous counterattack proved costly to a handful of infantrymen, who were skewered in their unprotected regions by spears or hacked to pieces by hand axes. For the Ordovices, however, the withdrawal proved even more punishing. There was simply no way to navigate past the rows of sharp stakes without exposing themselves to thrusts from both spear and gladius. Devoid as most of the warriors were of armour, the Romans' counter-strikes proved deadly. Then there was the matter of negotiating through the trench with all its obstacles. Numerous warriors who'd been injured during the assault were trying to climb their way back to safety. The fortunate ones were grabbed by their friends and dragged out of the ditch. Those too badly hurt to be moved were left to their fate.

A cheer erupted from the Roman camp as the auxiliary infantrymen caught their breath. Relief soon turned to anger, with several of their men plunging their weapons into the enemy wounded.

"Belay that!" a centurion shouted, smacking the offenders with his vine stick. "These fucking pigs will not be granted a quick death.

First, they will tell us everything they know and then crucifixion for the lot of them."

It was dark when Elisedd opened his eyes. He was tied to a stake atop a pyre; his wife, Runa, was bound to a second pyre and still unconscious. A ring of torch-bearers stood in a semi-circle around them, all wearing hooded cloaks pulled over their heads. Standing in the middle was a stern-looking King Seisyll and the dreaded mystic, Tathal. The high druid was wearing his finest white robe, bound in the middle with a bronze-plated belt. His hands and face were painted with a series of patterns in blue ink, except around the eyes, which were smeared black. And though he carried his long staff, it was the bronze curved dagger in his belt that captured Elisedd's gaze.

"You have failed us," said King Seisyll, his arms folded, his voice like ice.

Knowing he was already condemned, Elisedd became defiant. "It is *you* who have failed! We were under your protection, yet where were the Ordovices when my people were being slaughtered?"

"Aeron, god of battle and slaughter, rewards courage," Tathal spoke. "Had you and your warriors appeased him, you would have been welcomed into the afterlife as heroes. Instead, Aeron demands that those who cower before our enemies be sacrificed."

"A pit of vipers fuck your mother!" Elisedd snarled.

The druid gave a short, demonic laugh and turned to the king, who nodded. Tathal drew his long dagger. Torch-bearers stepped forward to ignite the two pyres.

Runa stirred as the wood started to crackle. The Deceangli chief would accept his own fate, however painful it may be, but the thought of seeing his beloved tortured by that loathsome druid drove him beyond breaking.

"Stay away from her, you unholy bastard!"

"Not to worry," Tathal said, a sneer crossing his face. He brandished his blade towards Runa. "It is you who have offended the gods. Your wife's end will be quick."

Runa's eyes opened, and her head whipped around as she regained consciousness. She cried out before coughing violently on the thick, acrid smoke. Before the flames could completely engulf the pyre, Tathal stepped forward and slashed his dagger across her throat. Elisedd gritted his teeth, tears streaming down his face as his wife's eyes clouded over, blood gushing down her chest.

"And now we must deal with the traitor," the druid said, running his fingers over the bloody knife.

One of his acolytes stepped forward, carrying a stone bowl.

Torches were set in the chief's pyre, the damp timber hissing and smoking. As Tathal stepped forward, Elisedd spat at him defiantly. The high druid smirked and plunged the point of the curved dagger into his stomach. The blade was extremely sharp. With a quick upward slash, he disembowelled his prey. Elisedd tried to gasp as his guts spilled from his torso. With a sickening splat a pile landed in the bowl, which the acolyte set to the side, allowing the flames to cook its contents. The flames started to lick higher, and a hot cloud of smoke billowed right into the chief's face. With the last of his energy, he sucked in his final breath, searing his lungs and sending him to join his wife in the afterlife.

It was midmorning the next day when the Twentieth Legion and Indus' Horse returned. While both Governor Scapula and General Paulinus were filled with anger and frustration at having been so easily duped by Caratacus and his allies, there was still a substantial measure of relief. Their camp still stood. The auxiliaries had lost twenty dead, with another sixty wounded. They had slain over a hundred Ordovices warriors, while taking twenty wounded prisoners. Thirty more of the enemy's injured had succumbed to their fearful wounds, coupled by the outright refusal of the imperial soldiers to offer them aid.

The soldiers of the errant expedition set about re-establishing their tents and repairing the ramparts, while the senior officers met with the centurion who'd been left in command of the camp.

"The Deceangli chief and his wife were taken away," he explained.

"Did they try to free any of the other prisoners?" Scapula asked.

The centurion shook his head. "No, sir. In fact, I do not think this was a rescue mission at all. We were in the midst of tearing down and moving the stockades when the attack came. The Ordovices actually attacked the Deceangli warriors, killing a dozen or so before fleeing with their quarry."

"What's that over there?" Master Centurion Tyranus asked, nodding his head towards the wisps of smoke in the west.

"We saw flames coming from that direction last night," the auxilia centurion explained. "The trees are thick that way. If it was a campfire, it was an awfully big one. I thought it might be a trap meant to lure us away from the camp."

Scapula turned to Julianus. "Take two hundred men and find the source of that smoke."

"I'll go with them," Magnus said, drawing confused stares from a handful of his peers. "I think I know what it is...and it's not a campfire."

"In the meantime, we should get a little information from the Ordovices prisoners before we dispose of them," General Paulinus remarked.

Commander Julianus sent sections of his horsemen ahead in skirmishing formation, in case they should come across stray bands of enemy warriors. Centurion Magnus rode with him at the centre of the column.

"What is it you suspect?" the cavalry officer asked. He had only taken over the regiment a year prior and was not as familiar with the indigenous tribes as the centurion.

"It's just a hunch," Magnus replied. "The raid was not a rescue mission, since they slew some of their allied warriors. Nor did they try to overrun the garrison or attack our food stores. The Deceangli chief and his wife were taken for a reason, and it's not because they were being rescued." He paused as they reached the wood line. The smoke was now more noticeable. "I saw something once, during the invasion..."

"Commander Julianus!" The trooper's shout alerted the officers.

They rode through the trees to where a section of horsemen gathered in a small opening in the woods. Magnus and the cavalry officer dismounted as they came upon the macabre scene.

The bodies of Elisedd and Runa were badly charred, their faces mostly burned away and scarcely recognisable. Flies gathered around the pile of burned guts in a stone bowl on the pyre. Much of the wood was damp and unsinged.

"They buggered off before the bodies were consumed," a trooper stated.

"Perhaps they wanted us to find them." Magnus observed.

"Is this what you expected to find?" Julianus asked.

"It is. During the invasion our chief tribune was captured, hung upside down, and disembowelled. A sacrifice by the druids to their foul gods. Caratacus has done the same to these poor sods."

"And by surrendering in the hopes of saving their people, the Deceangli chief and his wife sealed their own fate."

Magnus and Julianus returned and gave their report to the governor, who dismissed them without a word. Scapula then sat on a camp stool, waiting for his principia tent to be erected, his chin resting in his hand. The governor of Britannia was in a vile mood. He had been duped by Caratacus, who had escaped their attempt to engage him in battle. And now their prized prisoners had been burned and gutted by druids.

"I should have listened to you, Paulinus," he said.

The legate sat on a nearby stool, running a rag over his spatha.

"To be fair, sir," Tyranus spoke up as he joined them, "We committed a strategic error, but so too did our enemies."

"Explain."

The master centurion nodded towards the oxcarts where much of their rations were stored. "They had enough warriors that there is a chance they could have overrun the camp. Yet at no time did they attack our supplies. They could have easily set fire to the wagons and slain the oxen, leaving us critically short of food, deep in enemy territory. So fixated on avenging themselves for the perceived slight of the Deceangli surrender, they lost an opportunity to make life an even greater misery for us."

Though this assessment did not cheer the governor, it did bring a strong measure of relief. His face grew pale for a moment at the thought of not only losing Caratacus, but what would happen to his army if their food and supplies had been destroyed.

Paulinus said nothing, but continued to wipe down his sword, the corner of his mouth upturned in a partial grin. There were reasons why the centurions of the First Cohort were the chief tactical and strategic advisors to the commanding general. The centurion primus pilus and his four centurions primus ordo were the most experienced soldiers in the entire legion. They understood battle tactics, large-scale strategy, and the underappreciated yet crucial logistics better than any. Both he and Scapula would do well to listen to their counsel in the future.

It was not just the Romans who realized the opportunity lost. A day's trek to the southwest, the Ordovices raiding party found the main army. When King Seisyll told Caratacus and King Orin of his force's success, he was met with much derision from his fellow monarch.

"Your men breached the Roman camp, guarded by a handful of auxiliaries, and none of you even thought to destroy their supply wagons?"

Caratacus said nothing, though even he was flustered by Seisyll's short-sightedness. It was anywhere from four days to a week's march from the Roman camp to their territory. With no rations and little to forage, starvation would have weakened them considerably. Spread out along the rough mountains and dense forests, they would have been easy prey for Caratacus and his warriors. Seisyll, however, remained defiant.

"Our mission was to exact vengeance on the Deceangli traitors," he retorted. "The collaborators have been sacrificed, and we have the favour of the gods now."

The Catuvellauni prince folded his hands in his lap while the two allied kings bickered. It troubled him to see the alliance he had fought so long to forge on the verge of collapse. Relations between Ordovices and Silures had been hostile for a hundred years, and it stood to reason that each would seek any opportunity to undermine Caratacus' trust in the other.

Orin was right, of course. They had lost a valuable opportunity to destroy the Romans' food stores. Starvation was a powerful weapon. And yet, Caratacus was a deeply spiritual man, who trusted in the counsel of Tathal and the other druids. If a sacrifice to Aeron was demanded, would not the god of slaughter grant them far greater victories than a few burned sacks of Roman grain?

"Enough!" he roared, leaping to his feet. His eyes were wide, his face red with anger. "We will *not* lose all we have fought for over a petty squabble such as this. We may have lost an opportunity to starve our enemies, but we killed their soldiers and offered up the traitorous Elisedd and his bitch of a wife to the gods." He then looked at the chief druid, who'd been standing by idly, leaning against his staff. "Tathal, does Aeron favour us now? Did our sacrifice please him?"

Tathal nodded slowly. "It does, Prince of Catuvellauni. But his favour is fleeting, for he laments seeing his children torn in bitterness against each other. He would just as soon abandon us, should we not prove our worth by standing together as one."

"Then that is what we will do," Caratacus said with grim determination. "If we are to defeat the Romans, our armies must not be divided by tribal or racial lines, but united under one banner."

"And who will lead them?" Seisyll asked. "Which of the kings is most worthy, and will the other subjugate himself to the monarch from another tribe?" His glanced over at Orin.

"If your peoples are to be truly united," Tathal said, "Then it should be neither Orin nor Seisyll that leads our army."

Orin, surprisingly docile in his response, stood and took a deep breath, knowing what must be done. He drew his broadsword and knelt before Caratacus. "Caratacus, Prince of the Catuvellauni, my brother in blood who united the peoples of this land. You truly are blessed by the gods, and I pledge my sword to your service."

Seisyll was caught completely off-guard by this, and he nervously turned to Tathal, who bowed his head slowly and deeply. The King of Ordovices could not help but wonder if Caratacus and Tathal had staged the whole thing. He knew the Silures were beginning to favour Caratacus, and now their king was offering his supplication before the exiled Catuvellauni prince. Whatever Seisyll's doubts, it was he who had performed the sacrifice to Aeron, and with Tathal giving his blessing. He knew his only options were to submit to Caratacus or break off the alliance completely. Given that his own warriors would have his head for such blasphemy, there really was no choice at all.

"I also pledge my life and people," he said, drawing his blade slowly. "But I will not submit to a mere warlord or exiled prince. If Caratacus is to lead us, then he must be proclaimed High King over all our peoples."

The chief druid smiled broadly and proclaimed, "So let it be done."

Chapter VIII: Chasing Ghosts

The Ogwen Valley
10 August 48 A.D.
***

With Caratacus having disappeared, Scapula dispatched Commander Julianus and two companies of horsemen to find General Paetus. The Twentieth Legion and the remaining auxiliaries remained in camp, waiting for Legio IX and the rest of the division to join them. The governor was beginning to regret the course he had set his army on. Their inability to draw Caratacus into a decisive engagement, the loss of their most prized prisoners, plus the delay while waiting for General Paetus had cost them. Under torture, the Ordovices raiders captured confirmed that Caratacus had taken his army to the southwest. The Romans thanked them for this intelligence by whipping each man until the flesh was practically flayed from his body. When each was a bloodied wreck within inches of death's door, they were drug to the ridgeline overlooking the sea and crucified. A few days later, with the campaign season growing long, General Paetus and the Ninth Legion arrived. Having united their two divisions, the imperial army began the pursuit of their ever elusive foe.

Scouts, both native allied cavalrymen as well as troopers from Indus' Horse, provided the main reconnaissance for the army. The land was heavily forested, while what open terrain there was consisted of either rolling grasslands or farm fields. Large towns and villages were non-existent, and what settlements they did come across were hastily abandoned at the sight of the oncoming legions. In order to punish the people and deplete Caratacus of food, while supplementing his own army's rations, Scapula ordered every settlement razed, and all grain and fresh vegetables confiscated by his troops. As it was late summer, with the harvest approaching soon, the army was ordered to trample and destroy as many crops as they could.

During one such destructive raid, near the base of the mountains that lead into a place known as the Ogwen Valley, the governor and his legates sat astride their horses, watching as their army marched past where a single cohort set fire to the handful of huts and grain silo. Their translator, Landon, was stone-faced as he watched the settlement burn. The Silures and Ordovices were natural enemies of the Brigantes, and he found it unnatural to pity these people. Yet, he found himself stricken by pangs of guilt for the numerous women and children who would likely starve to death during the coming winter.

"I only hope this goads Caratacus into a fight," Paetus muttered as he spat on the ground. He turned towards Paulinus. "At least you lot got to bloody your blades a bit. We've done nothing except chase fucking ghosts this entire campaign."

For Centurion Magnus, there was a great deal of trepidation as the First Cohort passed the burning settlement and began its advance through a narrow canyon that led between two large, forested hills. The centurion primus ordo dismounted his horse and hefted his shield, keeping close to the lead element of his legionaries.

"Expecting something bad, sir?" a soldier asked, his nervous expression telling of his own forebodings.

"Just don't want to make myself an easy target," Magnus replied.

The Ninth Legion had taken the lead, followed by several cohorts of auxilia infantry, along with attached archers. The rest of the auxilia, accompanied by most of the cavalry, followed the Twentieth Legion. The trail was very narrow, only allowing three soldiers to walk abreast. The foliage and undergrowth were thick, making it impractical to pass directly through the woods. With almost twenty-one thousand troops, plus pack animals and baggage trains, the column extended nearly ten miles from end-to-end. And with no viable intelligence as to how large Caratacus' army was or where they might be, each crossing through the woods became a nerve-wracking ordeal. As they continued onward, not a sound was heard, aside from the tweeting of birds, crashing of an occasional deer or fox through the brush, and an unseen flowing river somewhere off to their right. Nervousness soon turned to tedium, however, with many legionaries grumbling the same sentiments as General Paetus. They would rather the barbarians attack than simply chase phantoms all over western Britannia.

Approximately a mile into their trek, the woods opened up into a meadow where the sun was breaking through the incessant clouds. It was now late August, and though the rains had been a nuisance through the spring and early summer, they had lessoned considerably over the past month. The sun had shone its face at least every other day. When one took in the various trees, shrubberies, grasslands, rolling hills, not to mention the river which bisected the meadow, the land was actually quite beautiful. Still, Magnus was dismayed to see that the woods converged once more, less than a mile up ahead. From well within that far forest of thick trees, the sounds of war horns emanated.

"*Contact front!*" the Norseman bellowed over his shoulder, as dozens of auxilia troopers near far the wood line were seen racing into the fray.

"First Cohort, make ready!" Master Centurion Tyranus shouted, riding up on his horse.

Packs and traveling cloaks were dropped, javelins hefted. The rest of the column halted as word passed that the auxiliaries, and possibly the Ninth Legion, were under attack. Given the thickness of the woods and undergrowth on the other side of the meadow, there simply was not enough room for the rest of the legion to manoeuvre. The First Cohort would be advancing on its own. They were in little more than a modified column, thirty men abreast and nearly as many ranks deep.

His gladius drawn, Magnus gave the order for his century to advance. They approached the woods at the head of the column. He could hear the sound of shouted orders, as well as the occasional cry from the wounded.

"Magnus, take your century left and clear those woods!" Tyranus shouted, practically leaping from his horse. "The Fifth Century will follow. I'll take the rest of the cohort right, just over the river."

"Understood," the Norseman acknowledged.

Much to his dismay, it was nothing but woods of such density, with a cacophony of undergrowth and sticker bushes, that his century's advance ground almost to a halt. Shields and javelins seemed to catch on every branch, and soldiers were unable to see more than a few feet in front of their faces. Soon any sense of formation became practically non-existent, and it was impossible to so much as see anyone on their left or right. After almost ten minutes of struggling through the brambles, with legionaries spewing forth a barrage of profanities, Magnus stumbled into an auxilia soldier. The two quickly turned to face each other, each breathing a sigh of relief laced with disappointment, at seeing they had run into their own troops.

"The enemy's buggered off," an auxilia centurion said, walking over to the Norseman. "You'll never catch them in this shit."

Magnus glumly turned to face his men. "Withdraw!" he shouted, blowing hard on his whistle.

The anger and vulgar barks from his men only worsened as they worked their way back the way they had come. They emerged from the treeline just as Master Centurion Tyranus was spotted splashing his way across a shallow fording point in the river.

"Bastards seem to have all buggered off," Tyranus said, straining to contain his own anger and frustration at the situation. His face and hands were covered in cuts and abrasions from their futile attempt to smash their way through the woods.

"I almost stuck one our own auxilia troopers," Magnus added. "Their officers said the same thing; bastards have all hoofed it."

"I don't get it," Optio Caelius said, removing his helmet and pulling twigs and leaves from his bent crest. "If they had us caught in a long column, unable to form battle lines, why did they simply piss off?"

"The terrain works against them as much as it does us," Magnus explained. "Caratacus knows he cannot bring his numbers to bear against us in this shit. He's teasing us, that's all."

Tyranus added, "And he doesn't want to face us in the open, either. He knows he cannot win a pitched battle against us. He hopes these hit-and-run attacks will break our resolve and we'll simply go home."

It had taken nearly half an hour for Scapula, the two legates, and the senior staff officers to negotiate their way up the narrow trail to reach the meadow. Tyranus gave them his assessment while they waited for word from the auxilia cohort commanders. The chief tribune of Legio IX made his way back to them a short time later with his report from General Paetus.

"We lost four dead and another fifteen wounded," he stated. "The auxiliaries were still assessing their losses when I passed by them. But from what I gathered, they lost roughly ten dead with thrice as many wounded."

Scapula asked his next question with gritted teeth, knowing the answer. "And what of the enemy's losses?"

"We couldn't even see them, sir," the chief tribune replied. "No idea how many there were, though it was likely in the hundreds given the number of spears and sling stones they were able to unleash in such a short time. Our men were able to form a defensive testudo, but only after the first salvo wreaked havoc on us. The auxiliaries were less fortunate."

"We've dealt with these types of attacks before," Magnus spoke up. "In the southern and eastern reaches of Britannia. Though the woods and undergrowth there aren't nearly as thick as this impassable shit. Still, the concept remains the same; we'll have to detach our light auxilia and skirmishers as flank security for the column."

"If we do that," Scapula protested, "we'll be lucky to march five miles a day!"

"It's either that or our pace is slowed by having to constantly bury imperial soldiers," General Paulinus surmised. "To say nothing of what it will do to the morale of the army."

"Fortunately, sir," the chief tribune remarked, "past the woods the ground opens up. The mountains are full of shrubs and grass, but little to no trees. It's simply too rocky."

This came as a relief to the assembled officers. Scapula ordered the rest of the column to push through with all speed. Though the army abandoned most of its artillery, Paulinus had convinced the governor to take a handful of empty wagons in order to transport any wounded who were unable to walk.

It took most of the remaining day to get the army through the woods, while recovering their dead and wounded. The absence of incessant rain had dried much of the wood, making the construction of funeral pyres much easier. Approximately three miles from where the ground opened up, following along the river, was a small village. What surprised the Romans was this one was not deserted, nor were the people running in terror. Cavalrymen screened the surrounding hills, while infantrymen surrounded the village itself. The governor, legates, and other senior officers rode forward to meet the local chief, who sat astride a tall mare. He was a middle-aged man with greying hair and beard. He wore a broadsword on his hip. Three pairs of spearmen dressed in mail shirts accompanied him.

The chief bowed to Scapula before speaking very slowly in his foreign tongue. It took Landon a minute to translate the words in his head. "He bids us welcome, but asks what brings the armies of the empire to his lands."

"Ask him first if he is not a member of the Silures, and why he and his warriors aren't with their king."

The chief puffed his chest slightly as Landon spoke to him. His reply was one of defiance and scorn. "He says Orin is no king to him. His people are neither Silures nor Ordovices…"

"The hell they aren't," General Paetus interrupted. "They have the same curly hair and darker skin."

Scapula raised his hand, silencing the legate, allowing Landon to continue.

"He pays King Orin a small tribute to keep his warriors away from these lands, an agreement the Silures broke recently."

"So they have come through here," Scapula emphasized.

The chief spoke some more, waving his hand towards the canyon to the south.

"Six days ago. Thousands of warriors. A rear guard of several hundred was left behind."

"That would be the lot who hit us," the governor grumbled.

Landon continued, "They said they were making for the peninsula to the southwest; however, the local chief's scouts reported they were heading due south, towards the sea river called *Mawddach*."

There was a pause as Commander Julianus rode up to the men. His troopers were scouring the hills for any sign of Caratacus' army.

"Have your men seen anything to corroborate this?" Scapula asked, after relaying to the cavalry officer what the local chief had said.

"That's what I came to report to you, sir," Julianus replied. "The ground here is so damn rocky, we have no idea which way they've gone. These hills are nothing but rock and scrub brush. They could have gone north, south, or west for all we know."

"Then we have no choice but to take this chieftain at his word," the governor said reluctantly.

Paulinus spoke up. "All the same, governor, we should take the chief, or perhaps one of his children, as a hostage. You know we cannot trust anyone in this cursed land."

Scapula glared at the chieftain who remained impassive. The governor pointed to him and spoke to Landon. "Tell the chief he is coming with us. If this is some sort of ruse, I will have his ass nailed to a cross, after we've burned his village to the ground."

Night came, and all was silent within the massive Roman encampment. Sentries paced the earthen ramparts under torchlight, while a cool breeze blew over the otherwise hushed camp. Most of the army slumbered. But in one centurion's tent, all was anything but peaceful.

Magnus bolted upright, nearly throwing off the heavy blankets on his camp bed. He was drenched in sweat, panting as if he'd just sprinted four miles. He sat on the edge of the short bed, his elbows on his knees, head resting in his hands, while his fingers gripped his matted hair. On these nights, he felt as if he were suffocating within the confines of his tent. He threw on his cloak and wandered out into the night.

It was past midnight, and a decanus was supervising a changing of the guard. New sentries had just been posted. The outgoing squad marched back to their tent, anxious to catch a few hours of sleep before the dawn. For Centurion Magnus Flavianus, sleep would once again be elusive this night.

Cloud cover prevented the moon or stars from illuminating the ground, and outside the glow of the sentries' torches, all was completely black. Magnus kept his cloak close around him as he stood with one foot resting on the mound of freshly dug earth. A pacing sentry stopped well short of him, and with a quiet, 'Evening, sir', the young soldier turned about and began his walk back to his post. The centurion's sleepless nights were no secret to anyone. Many legionaries had spotted him standing alone on the ramparts on nights when sleep escaped him.

"What can I do?" he asked quietly into the blackness. Despite being in a huge camp with over twenty thousand imperial soldiers, Magnus felt very much alone. And on nights where the darkness threatened to swallow them up, it felt as if the gods themselves had abandoned them. He shook his head slowly in frustration, uncertain as to how he could end his torment. He spoke to the night. "What will happen should I catch Caratacus, that ghost of my past? Or have I simply become a slave to fear…"

Chapter IX: Field of Sorrow

Near Lake Trawsfynydd
15 August 48 A.D.

Britannic Warrior

The chieftain accompanying the Roman army, whose name was
Oelwein, knew well which direction Caratacus and his army had
taken. The deception of compelling the village to remain occupied
was part of a plan put forth by King Orin. Caratacus understood the
Roman methods of terror and intimidation, and knew the people
would face severe retribution should his warriors fail to utterly
defeat them. Hence, he was reluctant to agree to Orin's plan of
allowing one of his villages to, essentially, be sacrificed to the
invaders.

"Oelwein fancies himself a nobleman," the Silures king
explained. "But he is nothing more than a peasant farmer with a
sword. By guiding the Romans into our trap, he hopes to win
himself a place on the high ruling council."

"Yet knowing the Romans, they will take him or his family
hostage," Caratacus countered. "Once they smell treachery, they will
kill him and send troops to wipe out his village."

"A necessary loss," Orin replied, with a dismissive shrug.

Seisyll scowled at him in disgust. "Such a contemptuous attitude towards one's own subjects," he rebuked. "Let his handful of warriors die in battle, certainly. But to betray his women and children to extermination is an act of villainy." He then looked to Caratacus. "And as our newly proclaimed high king, these are your people, too."

"Calm yourself, old friend. I have personally left a pair of guides with Oelwein's people. The only one who will be sacrificed is the chief himself. For his sake, his skill with a blade had best be equal to his pride and ambition. If he should survive, I may give him a place on *my* ruling council."

The Romans were getting close. Within a day, maybe two, the imperial army would be walking into a trap. Caratacus had been reluctant to engage the Romans in a decisive engagement, as so many of his warriors had already been compelled to return home for the coming harvest. However, the longer they waited, the more indignant his fighters became. While there had been universal acclamation at his being hailed High King of Silures and Ordovices, many of his fighters were beginning to doubt he had the same tenacity and fortitude of his slain brother, Togodumnus. His intention of beating the Romans down with a series of ambushes, while waiting for the following spring to face them in a decisive battle, had been met with much opposition. What pained Caratacus most, was hearing these same words of doubt coming from his own son. It was why he had finally relented, offering up a compromise that would allow his men to bloody their weapons without risking being enveloped and destroyed by the imperial army.

That evening, the high king found Jago sitting on a fallen log, well away from the camp. The lad had grown tall, strong, and had a sense of bull-headed determination that unfortunately reminded Caratacus of his youngest brother, Amminus. Yet at twelve years of age, he was still a boy, not quite grown to manhood.

"Will we fight the Romans now or do we continue to run?" the lad asked, as his father approached.

"We?" Caratacus asked in return, taking a seat next to his son.

Jago's gaze was fixed on the far horizon. "So many of our warriors have gone home, but what of those who remain? What of

Mother and Sorcha? Is it not both our duties to protect them? What would you have me do, Father? Though I am not grown to my full measure, I am stronger than any Roman."

"If strength alone were all that was needed, we would have driven the Romans into the sea years ago. I doubt neither your strength nor your courage."

"Then let me stand and fight with you!" Jago pleaded, facing his father. "Let me earn the right to be not just a man, but a warrior of our people. They have made you high king, and as your son and heir I must earn their fealty."

Caratacus was filled with conflicting feelings; fear that his son was not yet ready to face their enemies, yet also immeasurable pride at the lad's bravery. "I think it is time for both of us to earn our adopted people's trust and fidelity."

There had been no sign of the enemy since departing the farming village, and Scapula was beginning to wonder if they had been duped. The local chief, whose name he learned was Oelwein, had sworn repeatedly that he'd seen Caratacus' army heading south. As the army reached the wooded grasslands further south, they saw few, if any, signs of a large force advancing this way.

"Why do they keep running?" Scapula asked in irritation, his gloomy demeanour contrasting with the sun-filled afternoon.

"Gathering allies, perhaps," Paulinus conjectured. While not as outwardly flustered as Scapula, the legate felt the same frustrations as every soldier in the army. He then reasoned, "As much as our food stores have been taxed, their situation must be even direr. These barbarians have no concept of logistics, and their campaign season grows late."

"Perhaps they are avoiding any sort of conflict at all this year," his chief tribune spoke up.

"That could be," his legate said. "However, I would bet a talent of gold that they will attempt to make a token stand against us this before going to ground for the winter."

Master Centurion Tyranus added, "If I may, sir, Caratacus does not believe in token resistance. They mean to bleed us; he's just waiting for the right moment."

Oelwein was kept close to the command staff along with Landon. Both men maintained their silence for the most part. The chief viewed Landon as not only an enemy Brigantes, but a hated Roman collaborator. Fear had gripped him when his king demanded he allow himself to be captured by the Romans; however, as great as the risks were, it also offered him the very opportunity he had been waiting for. A pile of legionary corpses, with the imperial army in flight, would secure his place among their people. Perhaps even Caratacus, named high king of all lands west of the River Sabrina, would reward him for leading the Roman army to its doom.

The ponderous army was now in a low valley with cavalry scattered along the ridges. The low lying track was the only place where the heavy baggage carts could navigate without being heaved over heavy stones every few feet.

"There is a river just beyond those hills to the south," a scout reported to Scapula.

"That is the River Dwyryd," Landon translated for Oelwein. The chief spoke some more and the Brigantes man added, "He says there is a very large lake called Trawsfynydd a few miles beyond."

No one noticed the sudden perspiration forming on the chief's brow. They were getting close...

The Britannic high king paced behind a line of warriors hidden in the dense undergrowth. The time for battle was almost upon them. His people needed a victory, and he would not send them home to the harvest empty handed. Their hands would bathe in Roman blood this day! Though this was more of a large-scale ambush rather than a decisive engagement, Caratacus had still committed thousands of men to bloodying up their enemies. Taking the route through the western peninsula had completely thrown their enemies off their scent. While the remainder of his army would be dispersing within a month, the Demetae tribe from the southwest had sent a contingent of over a thousand warriors to aid Caratacus, and to acknowledge their acceptance of him as their high king. The fealty of another, albeit much smaller, tribal kingdom was a boon to morale as well as Caratacus' standing.

The attack would be executed by three wings of fighters. The first would come from the woods along the north side of the lake and attack the column from the rear. The second, from the woods to the east, assailing the middle of the Roman column. Furthest south, using a series of deep irrigation ditches for cover, was the largest number of warriors. Their purpose would be to fix the legions in place, thereby giving their lighter troops time to destroy the enemy supply trains. And because this part of the plan involved the greatest risk, it is where Caratacus placed himself. It was also where his son would earn his place as both man and warrior.

Jago stood tall and proud, bare-chested, while his mother applied the blue dye in various patterns around his torso and on his face and arms. He carried a wicker shield in his left hand and his father presented him with a long spear.

"The greatest of warriors must earn the right to carry a sword in battle," Caratacus explained. "Return with the blood of a Roman on this spear, and the greatest smiths will forge you a magnificent blade."

"I will earn my place as a warrior and as your son," Jago said, snatching the spear from his father's hands.

Perhaps it was the blue paint or maybe a deliberate attempt to alter his voice but, to Caratacus, the young lad seemed somehow older. And though he may have lacked in years, the suffering, bloodshed, and courage shown this day would age him immensely.

The Twentieth Legion led the advance through the vale, and Governor Scapula ordered Paulinus to see if the lake would make a viable place to camp. They were about thirteen miles from the coast, and if Caratacus continued to elude them, they would have to soon camp for the winter. Would they return via ship, or fortify within hostile territory? Either would require much in the way of preparation and logistics.

Combining his two divisions would give them an advantage if or when it came to open battle, but for the laborious march across the forests and mountains, it was proving to be a burden. It was not just the sheer numbers of soldiers, but the scores of oxen-led wagons carrying food stores, thousands of pack mules bearing legionary tents and camp equipment, as well as several thousand horses for the cavalry regiments and senior officers'. All had to be fed and provided for each day. On many days, the entire column stretched ten miles or greater from end to end. Scapula mentally cursed his lack of foresight. He realized now that his army would have been better utilized, not to mention far more mobile, had he divided them into two or three divisions advancing along a similar axis but covering a much wider swath of terrain. As it was, they were simply walking in a massive line, waiting for Caratacus to get the jump on them.

The senior ranking centurions made more than the occasional mention of the poor execution of their advance. While they had sacked the occasional small village or farming settlement, there could be countless others hidden behind the hills and forests they passed. Troubling as it was to Centurion Magnus, with the vanguard approaching the lake, his focus was on the task at hand. There was a vast forest to the right, which was now being scoured by auxilia light infantry. Two cavalry regiments rode ahead to screen the army's approach, while the men of Legio XX advanced on the road leading through a small strand of trees off the northeast corner of the lake.

In the eastern woods, Seisyll held his breath in anticipation. He watched the long column of imperial soldiers marching briskly along. He kept his warriors about two hundred meters away from the path behind a long defilade. The grove was not very large, perhaps a hundred meters from end-to-end, and the Romans likely didn't think it was occupied. At least, that is what the Ordovices king suspected, for not a single legionary or auxilia trooper was seen crawling through the woods to check for enemy fighters.

Further south, Caratacus and his bands of Silures warriors laid low in the deep trenches. Most were up to their chests in water as they hugged the grassy embankment. With the reeds and tall grasses covering much of the landscape, it was difficult to tell the canals were there at all. The high king looked to his right and saw his son up to his waist in slow-flowing water, clutching his spear as well as a handful of turf to pull himself out of the trench. Jago's eyes were closed. He was breathing slowly and deeply through his nose. He accepted that death was a possibility this day; his only concern now was fighting bravely, proving to his father and fellow warriors that he was worthy of being counted as one of them.

The Roman cavalry had ridden well ahead of the main column and were now out of sight. This made Caratacus a bit nervous. He quietly passed word to his war leaders to keep a watchful eye, in case they returned. The lead cohort of legionaries was just passing Caratacus' position, completely oblivious to his presence. A foreign war horn sounded to the north. The high king gritted his teeth in frustration. King Orin's forces, north of the lake, had either launched their attack too soon, or were discovered by imperial scouts. Whatever the cause, he knew he needed to spring the remainder of the trap now.

"Down with tyranny!" he roared, leaping from the canal, his sword held high.

Auxilia skirmishers had indeed spotted the force of barbarians lurking in the woods along the north side of the lake. This prompted those to the east to attack well before the entire army was within the trap. Instead of facing legionaries, the Ordovices surged from the eastern woods coming face-to-face with numerous cohorts of auxilia infantry. With spears and shields together, the imperial soldiers quickly turned to face this new threat. Up the road, Governor Scapula was pointing towards the northern woods with his spatha, shouting orders to General Paetus and the Ninth Legion. The discovery of these potential ambushers allowed them to deploy into battle ranks before assaulting the wood line. Three of their cohorts were directed to the left, to hit the Ordovices in the flank.

Meanwhile, the lead elements of Legio XX faced the enraged barbarian standing atop the canal bank. None realized this maddened berserker was the very man they had been pursuing these past months.

"Contact left!" Master Centurion Tyranus shouted, jumping from his horse and waving the aquilifer to him. The primus pilus

placed his century at the centre of the cohort, with Furius and Magnus on his right, and the remaining two centuries on his left.

As his men dropped their packs and formed into six ranks, the Norseman spotted a large force of barbarians emerging to the Romans' right. *"Furius!"* he called out. "We're about to be flanked!"

"Pivot your century off me!" his fellow primus ordo shouted back. "We'll anchor this point while you secure the flank."

Magnus raised his gladius high. *"Third Century, right wheel...march!"*

With precision brought on by many years in the ranks, the hundred and sixty legionaries of Magnus' century pivoted backwards. Optio Caelius made certain their extreme left remained close to Furius' right. Magnus had his men form a forty-five degree angle off their companions on the left. They only had moments to react, and the barbarians were now charging straight for them, rather than trying to manoeuver further around their flank.

"First and second ranks...javelins, throw!"

There was scarcely enough time for his men to unleash their heavy pila before their adversaries smashed into the shield wall. The Silures' initial charge lost much of its momentum, as scores of fighters were struck down by the fearful missile barrage. Men screamed in agony as their guts were ruptured and limbs mangled. Splintered ribs, arm, and leg bones burst through flesh in a gory display of horror.

Their own light spearmen unleashed a retaliatory barrage. Long throwing darts rained down upon the ranks of legionaries. Many of these deflected off shields, helmets, and segmented plate armour, yet a number of painful screams echoed from the Roman battle lines as spears plunged into the exposed faces, necks, and limbs of imperial soldiers. Fallen legionaries in the first two ranks were replaced quickly by their mates in the third and fourth. Those in the rear unleashed a second wave of javelins. With no armour and only wicker or board shields, the Silures warriors had little defence against these subsequent volleys. The first minute of battle had already been a bloody affair. The warring gods, Mars and Aeron, would be pleased.

For Jago, the time had come to prove both his valour and manhood. He tried to pull himself from the ditch, falling onto his stomach as the handful of tall grass he'd been clutching ripped from the damp earth. In frustration, he tossed his shield over the embankment and used both hands to pull himself over. His delay proved fortuitous, as many of those warriors who'd surged ahead of him were painfully struck down by the Roman javelin barrage. Some were dead, many maimed, their screams of agony ripped into the young lad's soul.

The broken bodies and hundreds of expended javelins obstructed their advance. Jago regained his footing as he retrieved his shield and raced into the fray. The initial surge of warriors pulled back a few feet from the Roman shield wall, having failed to break the line, leaving even more of their companions dead or dying. A subsequent volley of javelins flew over the heads of the imperial soldiers, though these were flung in a very high arc and were easier to avoid. Jago gasped as he leapt to the right, knocking a pilum out of his way with his shield. The shock of the weapon's weight jarred him. Thankfully, it failed to stick in his shield.

The young warrior took a deep breath and strode forward with purpose, maintaining his composure. He was now at the front of the throng of warriors. He steeled his mind, blocking out the piteous cries of the wounded. Jago's greatest fear was not death, but that they would be ordered to withdraw before he had the chance to kill a Roman.

He focused his attention on a legionary directly in front of him. What baffled Jago was how old the soldier was. He had always been under the impression the Romans recruited their fighters very young, yet this man looked to be three times his age. He knew nothing of a legion's elite First Cohort, whose soldiers were experienced, battle-hardened veterans rated the best close-combat fighters in the entire army. Had he been aware, it would have filled his heart with trepidation, or possibly excitement at the possibility of killing one of the empire's best.

"They're not pressing the advantage, sir," a decanus said to Centurion Magnus.

As he slammed the bottom edge of his shield into the stomach of the warrior he was fighting, the Norseman took a quick moment to survey the ongoing battle. The barbarians were bravely standing their ground, refusing to yield to the imperial legions. Yet they were almost tentative in their attacks. The assailing warriors most certainly had them outnumbered, but no attempt was being made to manoeuver around the legion's exposed flank. A few hundred warriors could easily sprint around the open meadow that lay between them and the lake, and threaten the Romans from behind. Such action would force them to break off legionaries from their rear ranks, weakening the entire formation. And yet, this bizarre stalemate continued to their front.

"What the fuck are they playing at?" Magnus asked his signifier, ever by his side, behind the centurion's left shoulder.

"I don't know," the standard bearer said, shaking his head. "It's as if they aren't even trying to win."

"They're simply holding us in place," Magnus suddenly realized. He gnashed his teeth at the revelation. "This is nothing more than a bloody diversion!"

As one of his warriors took a Roman spear to the ribs, King Seisyll lunged past the stricken man and plunged his sword into the auxiliary infantryman's guts. Though lighter and allowing for greater mobility, the protection offered by hamata chainmail paled in comparison to that of segmentata plate. The king's blade burst through links and ripped into the soldier's stomach. He wrenched the weapon free, bringing the heavy sword down upon the shoulder armour of another trooper as he stepped back and away. Though the layered shoulder guards withstood the blow, it unbalanced the soldier enough that he was quickly skewered by several spear points. And though the auxiliaries gave as good as they took, Seisyll and his massed horde of fighters was beginning to overwhelm them.

Despite their warriors to the north having been spotted and unable to 'close the trap' on the Romans, they still managed to distract most of the Ninth Legion, along with a sizeable portion of the cavalry and auxilia infantry who made up the rear guard. King Seisyll, having spotted the approaching enemy forces dispatched by Scapula, ordered two thousand of his warriors to face the oncoming threat of three legionary cohorts sent to flank him. The rest of his men continued their relentless onslaught of the Roman auxilia. Caratacus had also concentrated the greatest number of his skirmishers with the Ordovices. From behind their mates, they continued to rain down sling stones and throwing spears upon the imperial soldiers.

Because of the relentless attacks from the Ordovices, and because they were unable to cohesively form their battle lines, the auxiliaries were compelled to give ground, with most cohorts abandoning the road altogether. They were now fighting a chaotic battle in the trees and undergrowth of the woods between the road and the lake. Bands of Seisyll's men had even driven several cohorts of imperial troopers all the way back to the water's edge. Furthermore, they had split the Roman column in two. With both legions being held in place, they were unable to come to the aid of the hard-pressed auxiliary cohorts in the centre of the column, the three cohorts from Legio IX notwithstanding.

Sensing a better opportunity for his skirmishers, the king turned to the chief leading his light fighters. "Take your men and support our warriors on the right," he ordered. "They are facing legionaries and could use the help of your darts and sling stones."

A shouted order, the blow of a war horn, and soon several hundred spear throwers and slingers were rushing north to support their comrades, who were being hard-pressed by the onslaught of legionaries. An imperial observer would have marvelled at the discipline and organization of these men, who were certainly more than just a rabble of 'barbarians'.

Seisyll's intuition proved timely. Though storms of pila had left many dead and dying, the imperial soldiers attempting to smash through their flank had been checked by the stalwart courage and tenacity of the Ordovices fighters. A steady barrage of darts and sling stones soon compelled the legionary cohorts to close ranks, hunkering low behind their shield walls. And though his warriors had pressed the auxilia cohorts towards the water's edge, the ground here was more open, allowing them to close ranks and beat back the Ordovices' onslaught.

Casualties were mounting, with his warriors beginning to fatigue. As he smashed his sword against an infantryman's shield, Seisyll hoped King Orin was successful in his mission to destroy the Roman supply trains.

Patience, Jago thought to himself as he jumped away from the legionary's sword thrust. He kept the soldier at bay by continuously prodding with his spear. He hoped to catch his adversary in the face, but the man was too quick and skilful for him and kept knocking his spear away. Jago couldn't compel him to break away from his mates and face him like a man, either. These damned Romans were sticklers for formation and discipline. Attempts to goad them into single combat were futile.

Filthy cowards, the young warrior thought contemptuously.

This particular legionary was the third Jago had faced. Every few minutes, the Romans rapidly withdrew their front line replacing them with subsequent ranks. It allowed them to keep fresh troops out front while frustrating their opponents. Jago and twenty warriors had attempted to exploit the momentary gap in the lines, yet the tactic was executed with such speed and precision that the young fighter had almost been bowled over by the shield strike of a surging legionary. Two of his companions had not been so fortunate and were slain by stabs from legionary gladii.

His aggravation almost getting the best of him, Jago was worried he would have to face his father with a clean spear. He therefore decided to change his tactics. He choked up the grip on his spear and held it close to his side. Focusing his vision on the legionary, ignoring all other friends and enemies alike, Jago hunkered down and made ready to lunge. The soldier was shorter than he, and as long as he kept his shield between himself and the man's gladius, he had a very good chance of overpowering his foe by sheer force.

Hurtling himself forward, the edge of his shield clipped that of the legionary, and with his right arm he knocked the shield away, leaving the soldier's torso exposed. Time slowed as he grinned in victory. He thrust his spear with all his might, anticipating the feeling of guts bursting and staining the spear blade with blood...but then a jarring feeling ran up his arm.

He should have aimed for the face or neck, for instead of slaying his foe, his weapon had impacted hard against the chest plates of the legionary's armour and was deflected away.

Before he could pull his arm back, the soldier brought his gladius down in a hard chop, severing Jago's thumb and knocking his spear to the ground. His cry of horrified pain was interrupted by the shield blow from the legionary standing to his adversary's right. The edge of the shield caught Jago on the temple, sending him falling to the ground in a heap as he lost consciousness. He never even felt the sword thrust to the heart that ended his life.

Chapter X: To the Sea

***

Because the Romans had time to react to the botched ambush, King Orin was unable to launch his warriors' full might against their column of supply wagons. They had managed to kill the oxen pulling a pair of wagons before being compelled to withdraw; however, this would amount to little more than a minor nuisance to the invaders. But although they failed their chief objective, much had been accomplished by the raid. They had unleashed chaos upon the otherwise disciplined imperial forces, proving that with only a portion of their warriors, they could make the invaders bleed. Seisyll's warriors had the most success, striking the column at its most vulnerable point in the centre and inflicting hundreds of casualties upon the auxilia and allied cohorts. It was, therefore, with reluctance that the Ordovices king heeded the horn blows from Caratacus, ordering them to withdraw. The return of the Roman cavalry vanguard had necessitated this. It was only by a matter of minutes that Seisyll and his fighters escaped being cut off and surrounded by imperial horsemen. The high king and his men were able to make their way through the canals and trenches before cavalry or legionaries could conduct any sort of pursuit. Yet despite the overall success of the raid, for Caratacus there was no joy to be had that night. His son was missing.

Eurgain sat with her arms wrapped around her knees, gazing into the fire. Little Sorcha sat with her mother, her head resting on her shoulder. A tear rolled down her cheek, and she feared the worst for her big brother. The high queen found it perverse that hosts of warriors drank and celebrated, while their prince was missing and presumed dead. And what *had* happened to Jago? Several warriors said they saw the brave young fighter leap at the Roman lines, but then he seemed to disappear.

"My son is with my ancestors," Caratacus said, with as much stoicism as he could muster.

"You don't know that," his wife protested.

"I doubt the Romans are taking prisoners," he reasoned. "I know he fell bravely like a true Catuvellauni. If only our people had even a small measure of his courage..." He nearly choked on his words, sniffing hard and fighting the tears that threatened to fall. His wife and daughter embraced him as he struggled with his overwhelming sorrow. He knew he should be proud of Jago who, after four years of Roman oppression, had finally fought to liberate his people in battle. Caratacus cursed himself for not beginning the lad's training much sooner. He should have known that the day Jago would have to face the Romans in battle would come sooner rather than later. It was his fault his son dead, and it would forever be his greatest failure.

For the Romans, there was much confusion during the battle's aftermath. Scapula and his commanding officers grappled with the slew of conflicting reports to discern what exactly had transpired. Clearly they had been ambushed, with the centre of the column suffering the worst in terms of casualties. And yet, the barbarians failed to trap them completely, perhaps because their numbers were simply too few. Both General Paetus and Commander Julianus had cautioned against presuming Caratacus' army was smaller than anticipated.

"The campaign season grows late, and many of their fighters may have gone home," the cavalry officer reckoned.

Paetus nodded towards the numerous corpses that lined the northern shoreline, where the Ninth Legion had done some of its fiercest fighting. "They abandoned so many of their dead and wounded. But given the losses we sustained, can either side really call this a victory?"

Legionaries were walking along, plunging their blades into any wounded barbarian they found.

"The dead know not whether their side won or lost," Paulinus said quietly, as he watched scores of legionaries and auxilia troopers dragging away the bodies of their fallen.

"We'll camp here tonight," Scapula ordered.

"Very good," Paulinus said, with a relieved sigh. "We should also give the men a day to bid proper farewell to their fallen mates."

The governor bobbed his head lazily in acceptance. He was clearly exhausted, both physically and emotionally. He was feeling the strain of his numerous poor decisions and hated that he had to content himself that their losses were not more severe. And though it was the enemy who had fled, he clearly did not feel as if he had won anything close to what one would consider a victory.

Just past the southern edge of the lake, Magnus and the rest of the First Cohort's officers finished tallying their own loses. Seven were dead, another twenty-eight wounded.

"Regrettable but acceptable," Master Centurion Tyranus acknowledged, as he read the reports from his centurions primus ordo. "We could have easily fared much worse."

"The auxiliaries in the centre of the column took a beating," Centurion Furius noted. "And I heard from a mate in the Ninth that they had a bastard of a time with those cock-eaters in the woods."

Magnus concurred. "At least we were able to fight our adversaries in the open. Still, I am troubled as to why they did not press us harder. There was no manoeuver, no attempt to flank us, just a toe-to-toe battering against our shield wall."

"They weren't trying to defeat us," came the voice of Legate Paulinus, as he walked over to his senior leaders.

"General, sir," Tyranus said.

He and the rest of the centurions rose to their feet. Paulinus waved for them to sit down and set his camp stool next to them.

"What have we found out from the prisoners?" a centurion asked.

"I'll give those bastards credit, they are difficult to break," the legate said, avoiding the question for a moment. "Torture is tricky. One needs to get them to talk without breaking them to the point they start spouting off a bunch of shit, just to make it stop."

The centurions chuckled grimly.

The general continued, "We believe they were after our supplies. Thankfully, our skirmishers discovered one phase of their ambush north of the lake. Had they been able to catch the army strung out in the woods, they could have very easily destroyed most of our food stores and supply wagons. A credit to the auxilia cohorts who closed ranks around our stores. They took a severe punishing, but they held."

Tyranus remarked, "Caratacus knows his chances of besting us in battle are minimal, at least not without suffering thousands of losses. By attempting to starve us out, they minimize the risk to their warriors. He is clever, I'll give him that."

"He's also been named High King of both Silures and Ordovices."

Paulinus' remark caused the centurions to stare at him wide-eyed.

"The barbarian prisoners were only too happy to share that little piece of information. Some even refer to him as 'High King of Britannia'."

"As high king, he keeps all the tribes united," Tyranus grumbled.

"It also means they will be more likely to fracture should we capture or kill him," Magnus observed. He looked to Paulinus. "But what happens now, sir?"

"Now, we take a day to honour our dead. The day after tomorrow, we make our way towards the sea. Scouts have returned, and it seems Caratacus has buggered off completely, putting as many miles between his ass and us as he could. With as many wounded as we've suffered, pursuit is impossible at this point. Wagons are overflowing, and we're going to need to get creative in how we transport the rest."

The legate went on to explain that the army would back-track about three miles up the road they had come down before making their way west, following the river to the sea. From there, they would march south along the coast, searching for a suitable place to camp for the winter.

"No going home for us, then," Furius observed.

Tyranus then pronounced, "As long as we have a secure position to fortify, with supply access via the sea, we will be in good position to hit these bastards again, come spring."

The collective mood the following day was very sombre. Outside the camp along the lakeshore were rows of pyres. The surrounding region had been scoured for dry timber, and now the bloodied corpses of the fallen were laid atop in reverence. Each fallen man's century took the time to pay their respects, with centurions calling their names three times as their souls were sent on to Elysium.

Two of the slain were from Magnus' century. For one of the soldiers, Optio Caelius asked that he be allowed to light the pyre.

"It was the only death he would have found acceptable," Caelius said later, after they watched the flames take hold of the timber, crackling and billowing thick, black smoke.

"In battle, you mean," the centurion noted.

"Twenty-seven years in the ranks, he could have retired at any time. He confessed to me not long ago that he had no idea what else to do with his life, and it would be best if the barbarians got him before the army discharged him for being too old to wield a gladius in battle. He did not want to fade away as a crippled old man." The optio looked at Magnus with a sad half-smile. "You of all people should understand that, sir."

It wasn't meant to be a rebuke, though it certainly gave Magnus reason to pause. After all, the dead legionary had been a few years younger than he. And as the flames engulfed the kindling, he began to wonder what would happen should the army suddenly decide he was no longer fit to lead his men into battle. What would he do then? More than anything, he longed to find peace within his deeply troubled soul. And yet, he had no idea what would bring him solace. Perhaps it was the capturing or killing of Caratacus. He doubted it. Caratacus had not been anywhere near Mai Dun when Achillia was killed. No, this was not something as simple as a personal vendetta against the newly-proclaimed High King of western Britannia.

What Magnus did know was he missed his old mates more than ever. For more than two decades they carried each other through the harshest of conflicts and moments of unbridled sorrow. But now, every one of his closest friends in the legions was gone. Carbo and Decimus were killed at Braduhenna twenty years before. Camillus died protecting the legion's sacred eagle during the Invasion of Britannia. Praxus and Artorius left the legions soon after Mai Dun. Valens also retired from the ranks and ran off with Magnus' younger sister. Of all his old comrades, it was Artorius he missed the most. He had been more of a brother than friend since they joined the legion together at the age of seventeen. Artorius was gone, but there was one left. It was he the old Norseman would go see that night.

"Magnus, old man," Metellus said, surprised to see the older centurion entering his tent. The pilus prior for the Fifth Cohort had his armour laid out on his camp table, making notes to all the damage it had suffered, while his manservant polished various pieces of his kit.

"I needed to get away from the First Cohort for a while," Magnus explained. "Despite being in the same legion, I almost never see you anymore, old friend."

Metellus raised an eyebrow and chuckled. "So I'm your friend in my own right now, and not just the son of your best friend?"

The men shared a laugh.

Magnus reached over and smacked the younger centurion on the shoulder. "I would say I've considered you my friend since Judea. By Mercury, how long has it been?"

"Eleven years," Metellus answered quickly. "It was hot, dry, and the people were utterly insufferable...although to be fair, they really weren't any worse than the Silures or Ordovices."

"Difference is, I think these people will eventually be conquered. The Jews have been fighting for thousands of years. They simply refuse to acknowledge when they've been beaten, and I highly doubt that anyone will ever subdue them."

"And for it all, there is still something I miss about that place," Metellus remarked thoughtfully. "I can't say exactly what. But never mind that. You didn't come here to reminisce about the old days...or did you?"

Magnus smiled sadly. "I admit it hasn't been the same since Praxus and Artorius left the legion."

"And how long until you join them in retirement?"

"Anxious to be rid of me, are you?"

"I am, if I ever want to see one last promotion," Metellus answered candidly.

Magnus looked at him inquiringly.

He laughed and shrugged. "Come on, old boy, you're the oldest centurion primus ordo in the First Cohort. Hell, you're even older than Tyranus!"

Magnus did not reply.

"Every soldier longs to join the elite First. When we're at full strength, which I admit we aren't even close to at the moment, I have four hundred and eighty legionaries and decani, plus eighteen principle officers and five centurions under my charge. You have scarcely a third of that number. Your soldiers are all elite veterans who require little to no supervision. The youngest soldier in the First is still older than over half of my legionaries. You know how many pages of disciplinary reports I go through every week?"

"A lot more than I do, I reckon." While the First Cohort did have the occasional lapse in discipline, usually brought on by excessive drink, it was rare when compared to the rest of the legion. "So you want my billet in the First Cohort."

Metellus furrowed his brow. His next words dripped with sarcasm. "Hmm, let's see. Better pay, fewer soldiers to supervise, no fatigue details to oversee, plus you are all on the commanding general's advisory staff. What's not to like? Granted, there are no guarantees I would be next in line for elevation to the First Cohort, even if you did retire. There are other pilus priors who have seniority over me, though I hope my record will stand on its own merit. I will remain in the emperor's service long enough to see. If I am passed over, then I will be done with the legions. To be honest, either outcome suits me."

"Am I the only one who isn't certain as to whether I should ever leave the ranks?" the Norseman asked rhetorically.

Metellus' playful demeanour changed to one of seriousness. "Magnus, I have a family. Marcia never ceases worrying that I'll either be killed in battle or succumb to any number of infectious diseases. You see this gouge in my armour? Had I not been wearing it, I would have been spitted like a wild pig." He paused and took a deep breath. "And then there's my boys."

"How old are Lucius and Gaius now?"

"Seven and six, and. I feel I've missed too much of their lives already. I never knew my father—my real father, I mean. I was already a grown man when my Uncle Artorius adopted me." He took a moment. "I want my sons to know me, Magnus. My hopes at promotion into the First Cohort are as much for them as for me. Centurions primus ordo are ensured elevation into the equites upon retirement. I may still have a chance, should I retire as a pilus prior; however, that will take a lot of political manoeuvring, which I am not very adept at. But, should I manage to find myself as a member of Rome's noble order of knights, I need to make certain I have enough funds to ensure that Lucius can at least follow the career path of the equites. Marcia has already said repeatedly that gods forbid either of our sons ever joins the army."

"Yes." There was a long pause. Magnus pondered all the younger centurion had said. Metellus was only thirty-eight, and it would seem strange if he left the legions before Magnus.

Metellus saw the strained expression on his friend's face and was suddenly apologetic. "Dear friend, I do apologise. You came to me needing to talk, and all I've done is bicker about my own petty issues. Please, tell me what vexes you."

Magnus sat on the edge of Metellus' camp bed and stared at the oil lamp flickering on the table. "Family," he said quietly, almost a whisper.

"Come again?"

"It is family I feel devoid of," Magnus explained, coming to the realization. "I should have known it when I stood beside my brother aboard his ship. We've only seen each other three times in the last thirty years. The legion became my family, especially those I joined the ranks with. Artorius and I were, in many ways, still children when we enlisted. Praxus, Valens, Carbo, and Decimus became our older brothers. You still have a number of mates from your early days in the legion. But even when all of them are gone, you still have Marcia and your boys. My family is gone, Metellus…all of them."

The following day, many of the wounded who were unable to walk were loaded into supply wagons. Others had makeshift stretchers made from their cloaks with javelins used for poles. These were dragged behind their pack animals or by fellow soldiers.

Scapula first thought to crucify all of the enemy prisoners. However, with Caratacus long gone, there was no one to terrorize with the image of crucified warriors. He opted instead to have his men cut their throats and leave the carcasses to rot in the sun. The one exception was the treacherous Oelwein, who had survived an arrow to the back. The governor ordered him savagely flogged and then hung from a cross along the shoreline of the lake.

It took the better part of the day to make their way around the hills to the west following the river. They soon came to an open plane approximately two miles from the sea. The army was able to spread out into several columns, and they followed the coast another few miles before camping for the night.

Though there was at least another month of warm weather before the autumn rains, there was a sense of relief among the soldiers of Scapula's column. Scouts reported no signs of the barbarians since the Battle of Trawsfynydd, as it was now called. The terrain along the sea was a lot more open, negating any attempt for the enemy to set an ambush.

The following day they reached a tidal river so wide they had to make their way several miles inland, hugging a range of steep hills before finding a viable fording point. Still, there was no sign of Caratacus. It would be another two days before they reached their destination. Along the way they burned two settlements, taking at least a hundred sheep and other forms of livestock.

By midday, scouts had reached another large tidal river, with a large beach and wide open hills to the east. With only grass, scrub brush, and various white and yellow flowering plants, it was the perfect place for the vast army to encamp.

"At least there won't be any nasty surprises from Caratacus," General Paetus observed as he, Paulinus, and Scapula sat astride their horses on a modest hill overlooking the region. The legate turned to Scapula. "Governor, are you not well? Your face is rather pale."

"I haven't slept in days," he confessed. "Not since Caratacus got the jump on us. And I wasn't resting well even before then. We've had no contact with the rest of the province. I fear for what may have transpired during our absence. Will the restless provincials attempt some sort of uprising, what with half our armed forces trapped within enemy territory? And what about the constant troubles in Brigantes?"

"You've left your deputies in command," Paulinus reassured him. "When a province is at war, it is the governor's duty to be with his men. That being said, it would probably be best if you returned to Camulodunum for the winter. Not much you can do from here."

"Yes," the governor agreed with a tired nod. "Anyone know what this river is called? Or for that matter, where in Jupiter's name we are?"

"No idea," Paulinus said, shaking his head. He gave a sinister grin, nodding his head towards the shoreline. "There's a fishing village down there, perhaps we could ask one of the locals."

Scapula elected not to destroy the fishing village. Informing the local chief that they would be spared, so long as they provided fish for the army. They also learned that the river, known to the locals as the *Dyfi*, was south-flowing and therefore a good source of fresh water.

"It is a very long river," Landon reported to the governor. "It shares its watershed with both the Dee and Sabrina Rivers."

The villagers, thus far oblivious to the war, were absolutely terrified at the sight of the vast imperial army. Most had never even heard of Caratacus, nor did they know he had been named high king over their own monarch, Orin.

"They say Orin is not their king," the Brigantes interpreter added. "To the south along the peninsula is the Demetae territory. Their chief confesses he has no idea which side their king has declared for, if any."

"That's no surprise," Paulinus stated. "On this remote corner of the isle, no one would bother with a small fishing village such as this." He sniffed the air and gazed out towards the sea. "I have to say, this is quite the tranquil little corner of the empire."

Scapula looked at him with a raised eyebrow and grinned "Of course. All the lands of Britannia should be regarded as the emperor's. We should make sure these people are well aware of who they now serve."

"They probably don't give a damn one way or the other," the legate conjectured. "It's the same for most peasants throughout the world. A local chief or a foreign emperor, it matters not. Just as long as they are left to live their lives in peace."

Since they would remain in camp for at least the next six months, the legates ordered their men to build semi-permanent guard towers and other structures. Legionaries would still utilize tents for their quarters. A functioning latrine was erected with a sewage line directly fed from the River Dyfi. Each legion had its own separate camp. The auxilia infantry cohorts built their own between the two larger fortresses. Cavalrymen were housed near the sea with plenty of riding and grazing land for their horses. By early September, a reconnaissance flotilla of three triremes and a quinquereme spotted the camp, their commander coming ashore to meet with Governor Scapula.

"Inform Admiral Stoppello that we are establishing the army's winter camp here," Scapula directed.

"Understood."

The governor then looked to Paulinus and Paetus. "It seems I will be returning to Camulodunum a bit sooner than I originally anticipated."

"We'll still be here when you return, sir," Paetus reassured him.

Scapula nodded. "Confine any wintertime operations to reconnaissance and intelligence gathering. Perhaps we can make a few friends among the Demetae."

The weeks passed uneventfully. One afternoon, Magnus stood at the shoreline, arms folded across his chest, as he watched the approaching warships along the horizon. The Calends of November were nearly upon them, and the weather had turned decidedly cooler and wetter over the past few weeks. Though never cold enough to freeze, even during the dead of winter, the perpetual damp in the air chilled the imperial soldiers. Out upon the sea, the ships rose and fell with the tall waves. Rough surf lapped away at the beach.

"They're a few days early," Magnus observed.

"The seas get decidedly rough during the winter months," Tyranus noted. "Best we get resupplied now, in case they become unnavigable. Besides, we have some passenger cargo for them to retrieve."

"Passenger cargo? Governor Scapula left for the capital over a month ago."

The master centurion kept his eyes fixed on the approaching ships. A smirk now creased his face. "Tell me, Magnus, when was the last time you took any leave?"

"Just prior to the invasion," the Norseman answered. "Why do you ask?"

"Because four years is far too long without any sort of reprieve. You need to get away from here for a while, away from the army, the war, and hopefully that which deprives you so often of sleep."

"*That* will never go away, I'm afraid," Magnus remarked glumly.

"Perhaps. Perhaps not," Tyranus stated. "I do know sitting on your ass here, through the entire bloody winter, is not going to help you. I've already spoken with General Paulinus, and he agrees we need to place as many of our officers on leave as we can. The lads in the ranks have nowhere else to go, and so they can simply be given time away from their duties."

Magnus understood. He knew Metellus was hoping to take leave to spend time with his family in Aqua Sulis. Perhaps he needed some time away from the legion, as well.

"You had best pack your things," Tyranus said. "I don't want to see you return before the Ides of February."

Magnus returned to his tent and began sorting through his clothing and personal belongings. As he folded some spare tunics and socks into his pack, he wasn't exactly sure where he would go. It would take at least two weeks to return by sea to Ostia, provided he could find transport. Even then, little was left for him there. He had not seen his eldest brother in more than twenty years and didn't know if he was still alive. His grown nephews, he had never met. He supposed he could take a holiday to Malaca in southern Hispania. The weather would be warm and pleasant. As he leaned over his camp bed, packing his shaving and personal hygiene effects, the flap to his tent was flung open and a hard kick sent him sprawling onto the bed.

"By Freya's frigged tits, are you not packed yet?"

The voice of his brother, Hansi, turned his anger at having been assailed to one of bemusement. Magnus pulled himself off the camp bed into a low crouch, spun quickly on the balls of his feet, and slammed his fist into his brother's groin.

Hansi doubled over and collapsed on the ground, eyes wide and mouth agape. "G...good one, old boy," he gasped.

"That's twice you've left your man-parts unprotected," Magnus said, pulling himself to his feet. "The admiralty has a sense of humour, if they've sent you to ferry me away from this place."

"My last assignment before I return home," Hansi replied, pulling himself to his feet, hand clutching his crotch. "I get to take my baby brother on a little voyage before I depart for warmer waters."

"And where is it we're going?"

Hansi beamed. "Home."

Chapter XI: Heading North, Heading Home

The Northlands
November 48 A.D.
***

Having departed from the winter camp in the westernmost reaches of Britannia, Magnus was bound for lands few in the Roman world had ever seen. The first leg of their voyage would take them to Belgica. Ostensibly, Admiral-select Hansi Flavianus was being dispatched with an imperial magistrate to the Northlands, in order to secure a trade deal with an indigenous warlord. The magistrate, a rather fat, pompous fellow who was terribly prone to seasickness, was waiting for them at Gesoriacum, the very port from where the invasion force had launched four years earlier. The following day, with strong winds at their back, they came upon the large mouth of the River Rhine. A small outpost of a town, which bore the same name as the Gallic capital city of Lugdunum, seemed to stand watch against the forested barbaric lands to the east.

"The very edge of the empire," Hansi observed. "Therein lies the last bastion of Roman civilization in this part of the world."

They continued onward, following the coast east and northward. On the sixth day, they spotted a large river inlet. To Magnus, it looked the same as any other. And yet, there was a sense of familiarity he could not quite place. He knew he had been here before, albeit thirty-two years before.

"Is that..." he started to ask.

"The River Weser," Hansi confirmed. "The same river you lads took to reach Idistaviso. Seems like a lifetime ago, doesn't it?"

"It *was*," the centurion emphasized. "I was little more than an overgrown boy then. You know, I was reminiscing with Commander Julianus, about when I fought beside his regiment during the Rebellion of Sacrovir and Florus. It seemed like so long ago. Yet, the last time I came this way was even before that."

The flotilla made its way past a series of islands and veered north, following the coastline. They spotted the wide bay leading into another river known as the *Albis*. Magnus had heard of it during his years posted to the Rhine, but had never been this far eastward.

117

Another day of sailing due north, and the air became much colder. They were out in the open waters now, far beyond the reach of the empire.

"Worry not, Brother," Hansi said, joining Magnus on the prow of the ship. "The seas are a bit choppy, but there aren't any nefarious sea monsters lurking in the depths that can swallow ships whole."

"Yes, clearly Neptune prefers warmer waters," Magnus replied, wrapping his cloak around him.

"We should reach land by nightfall," his brother reassured him. "It's been some time since I've sailed these waters, but it is not difficult to find. I just hope we don't crash into any of the small islands or rock outcroppings that pollute the seas leading into the harbour."

Magnus gazed around, puzzled that they were the only ship on the water. "Where are your other ships?"

Hansi sighed and gave a mirthless chuckle. "Bloody cowards refused to sail past the Albis. We may dominate the waters of the Mediterranean, but on the whole, Romans are not exactly a maritime people. I hear even the Divine Julius about shit himself getting his little expedition across the channel into Britannia, a hundred years ago."

The waves became larger and choppier the further north they sailed. And though the winds were cold, they were not as frigid as Magnus anticipated. Land was spotted close to sunset. As a safety measure, Hansi ordered the ship to anchor in place, rather than try to navigate in the dark.

The next morning brought a chilly fog, and the ship could only creep forward until it burned off close to midday. Magnus smiled at the sight of the land that greeted them. High rolling hills covered in groves of evergreen trees, the highest peaks were capped with traces of late autumn snow. It was beautiful, magnificent, and strangely familiar to him.

"Our ancestral home, Brother," Hansi said, clasping a hand on Magnus' shoulder.

The ship found its way past a plethora of small islands, as well as jagged outcroppings of rock constantly pummelled by the violent waves. The harbour was really little more than a series of small docks and fishing huts, with a single long dock for merchant ships. Nets were hung between the huts, with fishermen gutting and cleaning their catches, while dogs and cats ran off with whatever they could scavenge.

The first thing Magnus noticed about the people was how big they were, even larger than most Germans he had seen. His grandfather, who had been short in stature, was certainly an anomaly among these giants. Fair-skinned like himself, they were mostly blonde of hair, though there were occasional redheads milling about. Most of the men had hair either to their shoulders or long and braided down the back. Long moustaches and beards were prevalent, although there were a surprising number of clean shaven faces. The women, many of whom worked beside the men, were tall and strong, with their hair similarly braided or hanging off their shoulders.

"Welcome home," Hansi said, as the two stepped off the dock and onto the sandy beach.

"If you say so," Magnus replied with a laugh. He may have resembled these people in size and appearance but he had been born and raised just outside of Rome. And while he often invoked the names of Nordic gods, in his heart he was still a Roman.

A dozen marines disembarked as part of Hansi's personal guard. The locals paid them little mind.

"How many times have you been here?" Magnus asked.

"A few," his brother acknowledged. He caught Magnus' inquisitive gaze and was quick to explain. "I brought you here to take you as far away as possible from what haunts you. What better place than the land of our ancestors?"

"And Admiral Stoppello simply let you take one of his ships on a personal errand?" Magnus asked incredulously.

"Oh no, the mission of establishing trade is very real. The hills here are teaming with iron and copper. The regional warlord is actually our cousin, Janne, who inherited the title from Uncle Gunnar."

"I vaguely remember him," Magnus replied, deep in thought. "Father rarely spoke of him. I do recall Gunnar thought Grandfather mad for abandoning his position as a Norse warlord to join the Roman auxilia."

They continued up the dirt road that led into the town proper.

Another thought occurred to Magnus. "Did you bring an interpreter? I cannot imagine you've picked up the local tongue over the course of a couple visits, and I doubt that our cousin, Janne, speaks Latin."

Hansi grinned knowingly. "You might be surprised. We've had a Roman liaison living here for the past four years now who's been teaching the chief to speak properly."

"Who?"

"Me, you sodden old bastard!"

The two turned to see a face Magnus almost did not recognize. The man was shorter than most of the locals with black hair that was greying on the sides, coupled with a darker complexion. Perhaps it was his manner of dress that confused Magnus for a moment. He was dressed in a thick tunic, trousers, and a fur cloak wrapped around his shoulders.

"By Thor's hammer...*Valens?*"

The old centurion responded with a laugh, rushing over and embracing his brother-in-law. "What? Did you forget I ran off to the 'old country' with your sister?"

"I wasn't exactly in a right state of mind when you left," Magnus reminded him. "I scarcely recall you coming to say goodbye."

"Given you were still in hospital, trying not to bleed to death, that's hardly surprising," Valens noted. "You were even paler than normal, if that were possible!"

"And Svetlana? She is here, too?"

"Of course." Valens smacked him hard on the shoulder, leading the group down a side road. "She is at the hall, as we speak. Hansi said that when he returned he would have a bit of a surprise for us. I never thought it would be you. I take it you have finished with your services to Caesar and the empire?"

Magnus slowly shook his head.

"What the fuck, old man? Are you waiting for the army to invalid you out, or are you that determined to reach Valhalla with a spear in your guts?"

"A question I am still trying to answer," Magnus confessed. "Perhaps my dear brother thinks I'll find it here."

For Cogidubnus, King of Atrebates and High Steward of the Catuvellauni, the days at his court were a frenzy of activity. His lands now encompassed the southernmost regions of Britannia, to include the Roman admiralty at Portus Adurni, as well as many of the lands that once belonged to their nemeses, Caratacus. These acquisitions had been a gift from Emperor Claudius to the man who had been Rome's closest ally in all Britannia. New lands brought him much wealth; a magnificent gift of stone and marble, along with the builders and craftsmen necessary to build him a magnificent palace just outside the Roman city of Noviomagus Regentium. At the moment, the palace was little more than a series of foundations with ground being excavated and tilled for the magnificent gardens.

Floor mosaic at the Roman palace near Noviomagus Regentium (modern-day Chichester)

The king stood admiring the construction work from across the bridge that spanned the channel inlet, just south of where the columns of the grand entrance were being erected. He wore a Roman style toga with the broad purple stripe of the senatorial class. The latest honours heaped on him by the emperor and senate had been the franchise of Roman citizenship, as well as acceptance as a peer of the senate. He kept his face clean-shaven, his brownish-blonde hair was long and straight, pulled back tight against his scalp.

"Sire, a rider approaches," one of his guardsmen said, nodding towards the north-eastern road that led to Londinium, eighty miles away.

"Ah, that would be our old friend from Catuvellauni," Cogidubnus said. He recognized the man's dark, curly hair, and the deep brown riding cloak and tunic he preferred.

The rider halted fifty feet from the king and his entourage and handed the reins of his horse to a servant, before striding forward boldly, his hand raised high in salute. He was a tall, well-built man in his mid-thirties. His black hair was short in length, though he kept it thick, in part to cover up his rather pronounced ears. He was still a handsome man, though his nose was a bit oversized even by Roman standards.

"Hail Cogidubnus, High King of Britannia!" the man said. Cogidubnus was, in actuality, only King of Atrebates. The Romans, however, had given him the moniker of High King of Britannia, granting him precedence over all other allied monarchs in the land. Even Queen Cartimandua was considered subservient to the Atrebates king.

"And to you, Amminus, Prince of Catuvellauni."

"I *was* a prince," Amminus corrected gently as he stood beside the king and admired the work being done on his palace. "My father revoked all my titles when I was exiled, and Caesar has yet to restore a single one."

"Give it time, my friend. You have only just returned to your ancestral home; a land in which much has changed since your hasty departure years ago."

"Because I did not fight alongside the Romans, like you, I am viewed as an outsider. And the same blood flows through my veins as Caratacus and our slain brother, Togodumnus. Because of this, our imperial friends regard me with a certain level of suspicion."

"Forgive me, but one can scarcely blame them," the king observed. "You could have returned with me when the Romans invaded. Had you done so, Emperor Claudius would have probably given you your father's hall and most of the royal lands."

"Perhaps," Amminus said, with a dismissive shrug. "But then I would have razed that filthy hovel to the ground, just like the Romans did. My reasons for not embarking with you are my own. But know this; I think my return will prove fortuitous to me and to our imperial allies."

"I understand Governor Scapula will be spending the winter at Camulodunum while his invasion force remains encamped along the western sea. When will you go see him?"

"Before the solstice," Amminus answered. "I need to make my presence known both here and within my ancestral homelands. I am certain you are aware that my brother has spies all over Britannia. I know of at least two at your own court." He glanced over at the king, thinking this would cause him alarm, but Cogidubnus' face was impassive. "My brother needs to know I am here, and that I intend to collaborate with the Romans. He is a great warrior of profound intellect, I will grant you. However, I also know he is a hot-head. Knowing that I intend to join the Romans in their quest to find him will drive him mad. His hatred for me will expose his weaknesses."

"Besides enraging him, how else do you plan to sell your services to the empire?"

"Simple," Amminus said with malice. "I am one of the few who knows what Caratacus looks like."

The imperial magistrate who'd come to negotiate with Janne over trade was still recovering from his dreadful bout of seasickness, leaving Magnus and Hansi to meet with their cousin void of distractions.

The high chief's hall was rather unusual, especially in contrast to the austere buildings that dominated the primitive city. The roof was triangular shaped with wooden shingles instead of thatch. A large walkway led up the short steps into the hold. These were lined by wooden columns painted red with white bases. To Magnus it seemed a crude Roman design made from wood, rather than stone and marble.

"It was Valens' idea," Hansi explained. "Janne hopes to trade iron and copper for marble and tile."

"Hoping to add a touch of civilization to this land," Magnus laughed.

Janne was about fifteen years younger than his cousins, broad of shoulder and thick in the chest. He was shorter in stature like their grandfather, Olaf. Magnus only had childhood memories of his uncle, Gunnar; however, he could see a strong resemblance in Janne.

"Kinsman, you have returned," the high chief said. He spoke in Latin. His accent was thick, making him seem rather foreign to Magnus despite their relation. Janne turned his attention to Hansi. "And what manner of Roman accompanies you? Is this the magistrate you spoke of?"

"Unfortunately, no. The magistrate is ill but promises to come see you on the morrow. This is my brother, your cousin Magnus."

"And I bid him welcome."

"And for that, I thank you." Magnus acknowledged, though his attention was no longer on his cousin or his brother, but on a rather striking woman who stood near the warlord.

She was tall by Roman standards. Her flowing blonde hair was kept off her brow by a bronze circlet and hung loosely down her back. Janne was quick to notice his cousin's distraction.

"I see you've noticed our Ana," he said, causing the woman to blush for a moment. "She is one of the finest copper smiths in all the land, not to mention a capable warrior."

"I have heard much about the men and women of this land," Magnus replied. "The strength of your people is legendary."

"*Your* people," Janne repeated, his face showing his confusion. He gave an understanding smile. "Of course. We may share the same blood, but you are Roman, like our friend, Tiberius Valens."

The sounds of a raucous scuffle caught their attention, and a rather well-dressed man stepped into the hall and began shouting and gesturing towards the commotion going on just outside the great hall. Magnus could not understand a word that was said.

Janne nodded and calmly spoke a few words in reply. "Apologies, my friends," he then said. "There is a dispute I must see to. Cousin Magnus, know that you are most welcome at any time within my home."

Magnus nodded almost to the point of a bow and took his leave. He first tried to leave via the way he'd come, but the main entrance was crammed with a mob of furious locals who were anxious to see their chief. He then saw Ana standing nearby. She tipped her head toward a small side door.

"Looks like you've made a new friend," Hansi said, slapping him on the back.

"Are you coming?" Magnus asked. "Or will you take your chances with that mob?"

"Oh, I'm going to stay and watch for a bit. Sometimes Janne will declare for one of the aggrieved parties. Or, he'll make them settle the matter by combat. Those are always fun to watch. Afterwards, I need to go check up on our poor magistrate. He'll be anxious to conclude his business with Janne and be on his way back to civilization. Although, he may not relish the thought of another weeks-long journey by sea."

Magnus took his leave and walked over to where Ana waited for him with the door held open. He found himself grinning inanely, and he gave a short bow as he followed her outside.

"Many thanks, my lady," he said, feeling awkward. He wasn't sure she understood Latin.

"It is a pleasure to meet you, at last," she replied.

Magnus smiled broadly in appreciation. Not only did she speak his language, her accent was far less pronounced than his cousin's.

"I assume you are… a friend of my sister's?" Magnus stated, half-questioningly. "Is it she who taught you to speak the Roman tongue?"

"Mostly, though I learned some rather colourful phrases from Valens."

Magnus laughed out loud. "That does not surprise me. I have known Tiberius Valens for over thirty years."

He apprised Ana as they walked down the snow-packed hillside away from the great hall. She was quite a bit younger than he, perhaps in her mid-thirties. He surmised she must be married, most likely to a great warrior.

"There is something you wish to know about me?" she asked, as they reached the large kraal where cattle and sheep were penned.

Magnus thought subtlety would be best. "I heard Janne say you are a copper smith. Does your husband share this profession?"

"He did," she replied. Her eyes suddenly filled with sadness. "He was a great warrior."

"Was?"

Ana dipped her head. "He departed this life for Valhalla four years ago this summer. We have been in a constant state of war with a neighbouring kingdom to the west, for as long as any of us can remember. My husband was killed during a raid. His ship was

125

smashed against the rocks. He made it ashore but was slain soon after." She paused and smiled sadly. "It would seem we have both suffered the same loss."

It was Magnus' turn for suppressed sorrows to surface. "Svetlana told you?"

"Valens, actually. He said your woman was very brave, and that she now sits beside Mars, your god of war."

"Our women do not become soldiers," Magnus explained. "But, Achillia was not your typical Roman lady. I am indeed sorry for both our losses. Did your husband leave you with any children?"

"No." Ana shook her head. "I had hoped to give him strong sons, but Freya denied us her blessing."

"Again, I am sorry."

Magnus felt more than a little uncomfortable; however, Ana simply smiled and nodded in acceptance. They continued to walk in silence. Magnus was uncertain where she was taking him. They came to a forest of evergreen trees with snow and frost clinging to the branches. Magnus wrapped his traveling cloak around him, pulling the hood up. He exhaled audibly, his breath misting. Ana looked to him, eyebrow raised. Whatever his ancestry, he was clearly not used to the cold of these lands in winter.

After some time of walking through the trees, they came to a small, open meadow. Magnus thought he heard the sound of rushing water. The ankle deep snow continued to crunch beneath their feet as they reached the edge overlooking a massive cliff. A gently flowing river wound its way nearly a hundred feet below. But it was the view across the deep valley he found truly breath-taking. The steep mountainside dominated the landscape. In the very centre was a massive waterfall. Magnus guessed it to be at least thirty feet wide. Torrents of water pummelled the numerous outcroppings of jagged rock before plunging into the swirling pool below.

"Have you ever seen anything like this?" Ana asked.

Magnus shook his head, his eyes wide in awe. "Never, and I have been from one end of the Roman Empire to the other."

They stood there for some time, the cold temporarily forgotten. Little was spoken, and Magnus could not recall how long they remained watching the majestic display. All he knew is that his mind cleared. For the first time in years, he found himself at peace.

Chapter XII: Consort to the Empire

Rome
December 48 A.D.

Julia Agrippina

The army of Ostorius Scapula remained encamped along the River Dyfi, while Centurion Magnus Flavianus, in his ancestral homeland, was being regaled by stories of the downfall of Empress Messalina. Within the Eternal City, there was talk of her potential successor. In order to help the emperor deal with his constant loneliness, Narcissus compelled him to seek out a dear friend. The retired prostitute, Calpurnia, was a surprisingly wise and well-educated woman. She and Claudius shared his bed during the years between his divorce from Aelia and his marriage to Messalina. Far more than simply one to help satisfy his physical needs, she had become a dear and close friend. Her former profession made any thought of her becoming his wife and consort absurd. This suited Narcissus just fine. And yet, there were growing concerns in the senate that a consort was what the emperor needed.

Narcissus at first protested, stating it had only been a few months since Messalina's execution. It would not be prudent to rush the emperor into another marriage. Besides, Claudius had a healthy son in Britannicus. Though only a boy of eight, there would be no issue regarding the imperial succession, providing his father lived long enough for him to reach manhood. There simply wasn't a need for Rome to have another empress consort. Much to Narcissus' dismay, however, Claudius agreed to hear the concerns of the consuls and his inner circle of advisors. The freedman therefore knew he needed to come up with his own viable candidate should the emperor concede to their requests.

"My friends, welcome," Claudius said, rising from his dining couch.

Rather than a formal meeting in the senate house or imperial court, he invited the consuls to join him on a large veranda overlooking one of the many gardens. The men took to their couches.

Consul Lucius Vitellius decided to get straight to the point. "As you know, Caesar, all of Rome was outraged regarding Messalina's betrayal," he began, while servants filled their wine cups and brought trays of assorted delicacies. "The people's love for you is absolute, and every last heart in the empire broke for you. The senate sympathises with your wish to not marry again."

"Indeed," the emperor replied. "I told Centurion Cornelius, if I ever married again, h...he was to run me through with his sword."

The other consul, Messalla Gallus, responded, "A noble but selfish gesture, Caesar."

This remark caused shocked expressions. Narcissus nearly choked on his wine.

Before Claudius could rebuke the consul for his cheek, his other closest advisor, Pallas, quickly spoke up. "He's right, Caesar, even if his tone was rather callous. An emperor *needs* a consort."

"But why?" Claudius asked, choosing to ignore Messalla's rudeness. "My U...Uncle Tiberius never remarried."

"Yes, and look how well that worked for him," Pallas responded, with a candour only he and a few others dared exercise.

Narcissus then entered the conversation. "Tiberius was an able ruler, yet so unpopular that the people rejoiced in his death. I doubt any empress could have helped him achieve the public's love."

"The purges following the downfall of Sejanus did not help matters," Claudius muttered, recalling the hideous slaying of the disgraced prefects children, who had been Claudius' niece and nephew through his second wife.

"Which only makes our point," Pallas stressed. "Think of what could have been prevented had Tiberius a capable consort, a Mother to the Empire. Why, the whole Sejanus treason may have been avoided! And the public's natural disdain towards Tiberius may have been tempered with the right woman by his side. Even the divine Augustus had more than his share of flaws. It was Livia who helped him retain the people's love."

"You perpetuate the myth that while Augustus ruled the world, Livia ruled Augustus," Narcissus remarked coolly.

"Rubbish!"

"No, it's t…true, to some degree," Claudius said, his voice calm and contemplative. "Remember, Livia was my grandmother. I was raised in the imperial household. I could be stricken blind and still know my way around the palace better than any. Livia was subtle but effective. She very rarely went too far, at which point Augustus would remind her that it was he who ruled the empire, not her. However, he also appreciated her candour and foresight. It was she who persuaded him to send my dear brother, Germanicus, to secure the Rhine frontier after that terrible disaster in Teutoburger Wald. Augustus wanted to send Posthumous Agrippa who, though my closest friend, would have likely gotten himself and another twenty thousand of our soldiers slain…" His voice trailed off. His mind wandered into the distant past. Such was often the case when his late brother was mentioned. Pallas sighed and rolled his eyes slightly, intent on getting the emperor back to the matter at hand.

"Then you have made our argument for us, Caesar. Marriage for an emperor is less about the man and more about the empire. Rome expects her emperor to have a consort who will share the burden of his labours. And if I may be so bold, Messalina's treachery aside, she was useless to both you and the empire. I'll grant that she gave you an heir, but that was the only good to come from your marriage."

Claudius was deep in thought. His chin rested in his hand. "I'll have to think on it." He waved his hand, dismissing the consuls and his advisors.

Only Narcissus lingered. Pallas gave him an inquisitive look. The two were friends, but as the emperor's most trusted advisors, they often found themselves at odds. Pallas was clearly vexed, for he was denied the opportunity to put forth his candidate. The two consuls shared similar looks of agitation. They, too, vetted women they felt would make a suitable consort.

"Something on your mind, old friend?" the emperor asked, once the others had left. With a tired smile, he rose from his couch.

Narcissus was one of the few people he trusted explicitly. Furthermore, he valued the Greek freedman as a friend. He sometimes wished Narcissus would, just once, call him 'Claudius'. As a former slave, and a Greek one at that, such a breach of decorum was something Narcissus could never begin to fathom.

"While I sympathize with my colleagues' intentions, Caesar, I am ever cautious about you rushing into another marriage. The consuls are noble men, and Pallas is my friend; however, each is likely to recommend a potential consort that will allow them to achieve their own personal ambitions."

"And you won't?" Claudius asked, his warm smile making the freedman feel more at ease.

"I don't *need* any more power or influence," Narcissus replied earnestly. "You have given me more responsibility than one could ever hope for. You even took my recommendation when I suggested Flavius Vespasian be given command of a legion prior to the invasion of Britannia."

"Y…yes, and a sound choice he proved to be. I was told many times that he and his brother, Sabinus, practically won the war by themselves."

Despite recent news from Britannia that the province was still very unstable, especially with the return of the formidable Caratacus, Claudius refused to let anything spoil the legacy of his triumph.

Narcissus was quick to guide the conversation back. "You demonstrated confidence in me when I recommended Vespasian. You trusted me when I told you of Messalina's betrayal. I ask that you trust me now." Claudius nodded.

Narcissus gave a sigh of relief. "There is one who has always been devoted to you, whose loyalty and love would be beyond question."

"Aelia," the emperor said, "Aelia Paetina." They had been married twenty years before, and she was the mother of the

131

emperor's eldest daughter, Claudia Antonia. Claudius had been compelled to divorce her after just three years of marriage, following the downfall and execution of Aelia's brother, the attempted usurper, Sejanus.

"She would be a good mother to Octavia and Britannicus, just as she was to Antonia," Narcissus urged. "Though Antonia now has a family of her own, think of what it would mean to see the union of her parents made whole once more." He then added slyly, "And don't tell me you don't still harbour feelings for Aelia, even after all these years."

"Fondness, perhaps," Claudius reasoned. "But it is difficult to maintain love after that many years apart. And b…besides, we both saw what a marriage of love did for me." His face broke into a scowl.

Narcissus feared he may have overstepped. "Well, if not for love, at least know she would be the perfect mother to your children, and to Rome."

"I will go see her," the emperor replied slowly, bringing the conversation to a close.

Far away in the Northlands, Magnus found himself spending most of his time in Ana's company. He thought his sister would chastise him, since she had seen so little of her brother over the years. And yet, she encouraged them both. Magnus speculated it had been Svetlana's intent the entire time to bring he and Ana together. Though possessing the natural strength and fortitude of her people, Ana bore little resemblance to Achillia. Magnus told himself it was better this way.

There was also much time for reminiscing with his old squad mate turned brother-in-law, Tiberius Valens. The two had been friends for more than three decades. Given Valens' rather sordid past, it did not surprise Magnus in the least to hear about his lascivious and unholy affair with Empress Messalina.

"To be honest, that harlot was more terrifying than any barbarian I ever faced in battle," Valens said. He swirled his wine cup gently, as he stared at the oil lamp on the table. His villa was furnished in the Roman style, which had cost him a substantial portion of his centurion's pension.

Magnus sat upright on his couch, his own cup held in his lap. "You know, I heard many rather unnerving stories about our late empress."

"Believe me, old friend, most of them are true. The tale of her working the brothels as a hobby, competing against a renowned prostitute and winning, all true. And, of course, her affair with Gaius Silius, whom they hoped would usurp our beloved emperor."

"Gaius Silius," Magnus repeated, his brow scrunched in thought. "Wasn't he our commanding general during the rebellion of Sacrovir and Florus?"

"That was his father," Valens corrected. "If he's still alive, he'll die of shame, knowing his son is the most disgraced traitor in a generation. And I don't need to remind you that I've done some pretty fucked up things in my lifetime. But at worst, I was a playful man-whore. Not once did I ever deliberately hurt anyone. Messalina used her *gifts*, for lack of a better term, to try to murder the emperor…Believe me, she was pure evil."

"It's not as if she's the first." Magnus shrugged. "Look at what Cleopatra did to the divine Julius, as well as the fallen hero, Marc Antony. In a way, she brought down the republic. Had she and Antony not tried to steal away Egypt, while personally insulting Octavian's family, who knows if the civil war and the rise of the empire would have happened at all."

"Well, your sister has been a constant reminder that women are not necessarily the weaker sex," Valens remarked, finding his perpetual good nature once more. "Oh, the beatings she gives me when I've been naughty!" He was now giggling, while trying to quaff his wine in a single gulp.

"Thankfully, I have long since gotten over my sister being just as twisted as you."

"That's a good thing, old boy," Valens said with a loud belch, before tossing his cup to a nearby servant. "But tell me, what of you and Ana?"

Magnus then smiled in a way neither Valens nor any of the old Norseman's friends had seen in years. "I feel as if she brings out the best in me. Just being around her has been a soothing comfort. I admit, I will be sorry to leave her when I return to Britannia."

"Piss on that!" Valens scoffed. "Take her with you."

"To Britannia?" Magnus asked incredulously.

"Sure, why not? She seems to be rather smitten with you. There isn't anything keeping her here. Honestly, if Svetlana had not fallen in love with this place, I would pack up and relocate someplace warmer, well within the empire's borders. The Northlands are beautiful, but the winters are too bloody cold for my liking."

"I think I understand why my grandfather left all those years ago," Magnus remarked. "It may have been nothing more than a change of scenery. He was a powerful warlord in these lands, yet he left to become an auxilia trooper in the Roman army. And as much as he talked about the 'old country', he never did return."

"Well, I certainly think Ana could deal with a 'change of scenery'," Valens persisted.

"There's still a war going on," Magnus reminded him. "The lands of the Silures and Ordovices are savage and unforgiving. You remember how hard those bastards fought. Try fighting them on their ground with nothing but forests and rocky hills. I'd hate to take Ana to Britannia only to wind up dead a few months later."

"Just give it some thought. I know your time in the legions grows short, whether Caratacus guts you or you finally decide to take your damn pension and be done with it."

Valens decided to let the matter lie, and returned to their previous topic of conversation. "You know, with Messalina dead, I wonder how long until the emperor's inner circle and leading members of the senate try compelling him to marry again."

"Yes, it will be interesting to see who the next consort to the empire will be."

"Make way! Stand aside for the emperor!"

Claudius reclined in his covered litter, fidgeting nervously. In the near eight years since becoming Caesar, Claudius had never gotten used to being accompanied by a full century of praetorian guardsmen everywhere he went. He found forcibly making their way through the streets, using their shields to shove onlookers aside, rather undignified. He had spoken once to his praetorian prefect, Lucius Geta, yet the next week it took the imperial procession two hours to make the one-mile trek from the palace to the senate house at the Forum. Such was the emperor's embarrassment at being so grievously late, he relented when Geta emphasized that shouts from his guardsmen alone were simply not enough to get the mob to make way. On this day, however, his nervousness had little to do with heavy-handed guardsmen.

"We're here, Caesar," Commander Geta said, his head protruding through the litter curtain.

"Thank you," Claudius said, accepting the prefect's hand to help him sit upright. Though he had only recently turned fifty-eight, the Emperor of Rome felt significantly older. The emotional trauma from Messalina's betrayal still lingered. Besides, he had never been in the best of health. His brother, Germanicus, had been a physical specimen resembling statues of the divine Hercules. Claudius, on the other hand, had been born both feeble and partially crippled. That he had lived to middle age, becoming ruler over the greatest empire the world had ever seen, was proof the gods had a rather eccentric sense of humour.

A section of guardsmen lined either side of the walkway leading to the home of Aelia Paetina. The rest of the century cordoned off the street, keeping curious onlookers at bay. A horn blower took a deep breath, ready to announce the emperor's arrival. Claudius placed a hand on his shoulder and shook his head. There would be no fanfare for this visit.

Aelia Paetina

Aelia strode towards the house foyer at the sound of the echoing knock. As her maidservant opened the door, Aelia was more than a little surprised to see her former husband, whom she had rarely spoken to over the past seventeen years. The last time they saw each other had amounted to little more than a formal greeting during the wedding of their daughter, Antonia, to Faustus Sulla. This had been, in no small measure, due to Messalina's jealously and closely guarded control over the emperor.

"An honour that you grace my house, Caesar," she said, bowing low.

"Please, Aelia, there is n…no need for formalities between us."

"Isn't there?" Aelia asked.

She and Claudius walked into the garden.

The emperor ordered his guardsmen to remain outside, giving him and his former wife some privacy. He followed her, taking a seat on a stone bench near the centre fountain.

"I have missed you," Claudius said, with a sad smile.

"Have you?" Aelia asked. Adding somewhat pragmatically, "You are Emperor of Rome and have not been my husband for seventeen years."

"Well…I never wanted to divorce you," the emperor said, hanging his head in shame.

"I know." The painful and terrifying memories of that time still haunted Aelia.

Her brother, Sejanus, had once been the most powerful man in Rome. When he betrayed Tiberius, the emperor's vengeance was swift and without a shred of mercy. Even Sejanus' underage children were killed, his daughter savagely raped first. The only reason Aelia had been allowed to live was because it was Claudius who had warned Tiberius of Sejanus' treason. He had still been forced to divorce her, with the emperor stating emphatically that no one from that treasonous line would remain a member of the imperial house. Both Claudius and Aelia had been relieved that Tiberius seemed to forget their daughter, Antonia, was Sejanus' niece.

"But you did not come to reminisce about our harrowing past," Aelia said. Shuddering, she tried to force those terrible memories from her mind. Her intuition told her the truth. She looked at him, tilting her head slightly to one side. "With Messalina gone, you need a new consort."

"So my advisors keep telling me. Of course, each has his own candidate in mind. Pallas was rather forceful, stating that for the good of the empire, I need an empress who could serve as a partner in my labours. He told me an emperor needs a helper, not a lover. He s...s...said Messalina was all the proof anyone needed that the heart lies."

"He's right you know," Aelia concurred. "His words may have been harsh, but they ring of the truth." She paused and pursed her lips. "But he does not think I would be a suitable consort."

"He does not." Claudius shook his head, which involuntarily twitched. "Narcissus thinks you would, though I believe he is mostly looking after my personal welfare."

"He is both loyal and a good friend."

"I was raised in the imperial household. I have survived the reigns of Augustus, my uncle, Tiberius, and my tragically disturbed nephew, Caligula. Behind the grandeur, it is a very cruel world. My grandmother, Livia, has been the only woman both strong and clever enough to survive as Empress Consort of the Empire. To hold any position of prominence within the imperial house, one must be cold, calculated, and at times cruel. You are none of these, my dear. I would fear greatly for your well-being were we to re-marry."

137

Aelia was not surprised by any of this. Even as an outsider, she had seen how vicious life at the imperial court could be. And as her brother and his family had learned, it could be deadly.

"Who will you marry?" she asked.

Claudius fidgeted with his hands, he resolve wavering momentarily. "There is someone," he said at last. "She is both shrewd and intelligent, though her heart amounts to little. She is as selfish and heartless as she is brilliant."

"And do you think it wise to share your life with such a person?"

"It is not for me but for Rome," Claudius insisted. "But there's more, something neither of us has any control over, and Pallas assures me will not matter in the end. Narcissus thinks it will prove disastrous, however. The lady in question is my niece, Julia Agrippina."

The winter solstice had come to the Norse lands, and Valens arranged for a Roman-style Saturnalia celebration at their villa. Magnus was fascinated to see that, despite the vast differences between cultures, many of the local traditions bore a striking resemblance to that of the Romans. Trees were decorated with bronze and silver ornaments, many commemorating the rebirth of the sun. Houses were decorated with greenery both inside and out. And given that Saturnalia celebrations often devolved into a drunken orgy, the indigenous nobles invited to Valens' and Svetlana's were only too happy to take part in the festivities. During this time, Magnus and Ana at last shared her bed. For the old centurion, this was the first time he'd felt a woman's touch since Achillia's death.

The Norsewoman lay with her head on his chest, arm wrapped around him. Magnus was surprised he was not assailed by feelings of wrongdoing or of having betrayed Achillia's memory. Such had been his fear. He had sometimes wondered if he would ever lie with a woman again.

Her eyes still closed, Ana seemed to sense his doubts. "Do you still love her?"

He confessed, "There is a part of me that always will. I have been haunted by the ghosts left in the wake of that terrible war; and not just Achillia, but all my friends who died a terrible death during my years in the legions. The ghosts of the past can never be forgotten. It is time I learned how to live with them."

Chapter XIII: Winter's Cold Embrace

Rome
January 49 A.D.

Empress Julia Agrippina with her son, Nero

The new empress consort was escorted to the altar by her cousin, who acted as the family matron. Narcissus was filled with feelings of revulsion and dread. The bride wore the traditional fire-coloured veil and plain white dress, belted in the middle with a corded rope. The emperor stood with the high priest, smiling more out of relief than any sense of joy. He had asked Narcissus to sign as one of the ten required witnesses. It was repugnant to the freedman. Not only was the new empress a woman he viewed as cruel and villainous, to say nothing of being the not-so-secret lover of Pallas, she was the emperor's own niece!

At thirty-three years of age, Julia Agrippina was a few years older than Messalina had been. She also had a son, who was three years older than Britannicus. This made Narcissus deeply concerned for the young prince imperial. He glumly accepted that Pallas, once his closest friend, had deceived and politically outmanoeuvred him. Narcissus thought most of the inner council would applaud his recommendation that Claudius marry his former wife, the Lady Aelia, of whom he was still fond, and who would have made a fine consort to the empire. The only other candidate mentioned was Caligula's former wife, Lollia Paulina. Her terrible reputation as an ostentatious woman with little smarts and extreme vanity, made her recommendation completely ludicrous.

Narcissus now understood why she had been brought forth as a candidate; Pallas had been coercing the other councillors for months, likely soon after Messalina's execution, plotting to have his lover named Empress of Rome. Every advisor and councillor at the imperial court chided Narcissus for bringing up Aelia as a suitable consort, decrying her as vain and useless. That Claudius had divorced her was also used against her, even though it was under extreme duress. It should have come as little surprise, then, when they all gave their support to Pallas' choice, Agrippina. Narcissus was repelled at the thought, and warned the emperor that the public would never accept an incestuous union between uncle and niece. However, in the end, Pallas and his supporters won out. And as the priest joined their hands, binding them with the ceremonial cloth, Julia Agrippina became Empress Consort of the Roman Empire. Narcissus, once one of the most influential men at the imperial court, suddenly felt very much alone.

The weeks passed, and January gave way to the Calends of February. The official despatches had reached Britannia, regarding the emperor's latest marriage. But the Norse lands, beyond the empire's borders, had been devoid of any contact with the Roman world. It was not until the merchant ship arrived with marble to trade for various metals, which would also return Magnus to Britannia, that news reached them.

Magnus donned his centurion's armour and made his way down towards the dock. The merchant vessel, now bearing iron and copper, was set to sail for Gesoriacum in Belgica. From there, the centurion would have to make his own way across the channel and back to Britannia. He and Ana walked hand-in-hand accompanied by Valens and Svetlana.

"A pity you could not come here during the summer," his sister said. "It truly is beautiful here and not so cold!"

"Summer is 'barbarian thrashing season'," Valens reminded her. He then embraced his brother-in-law. "Neptune grant you safe passage on your journey. And may Mars and Victoria guide your blade against Caratacus. Just promise me this will be your final campaign."

"One way or another," Magnus promised. "Once Caratacus falls, I will leave the emperor's service for good."

He turned and kissed Ana on the lips. She fought to remain stoic.

He felt her trembling. "It's not too late for you to accompany me."

"In another life, perhaps," she replied. "Come find me again when you are no longer a soldier of Rome."

The ship's captain walked over to them and addressed Magnus. "Centurion, we must depart soon or we will miss the tide."

Svetlana embraced her brother one last time, and the three of them wished him well on his travels. He followed the captain up the short plank. The ship was much smaller than Hansi's imperial warship that brought him to the northlands. Even the captain's cabin was small and cramped. For a few extra coins, he allowed Magnus to store his gear within and sleep in the corner. The centurion didn't mind. It was far better than freezing at night on the top deck. The ship soon lurched away from the dock. He leaned against the rail, eyes fixed on his family... most of all, Ana. He remained motionless until the ship passed the numerous rock outcroppings that dotted the harbour. He then closed his eyes for a few moments. When he opened them again, he wondered if it had all been a dream.

As they watched the ship slowly disappear on the horizon, Svetlana placed her hands on Ana's shoulders. "Why did you not tell him?"

"Magnus has enough to worry about, fighting Caratacus' hordes," Valens said quickly, before Ana could answer.

Ana then placed her hands on Svetlana's, fighting back tears as the ship disappeared. "There will be a time to tell him, but not yet."

It would be another three weeks before Centurion Primus Ordo Magnus Flavianus returned to his legion. At Gesoriacum, he was fortunate enough to come upon a cargo ship bearing food and pallets of leather procured for the army in Britannia. The seas were rough, and despite the storms that assailed their vessel, he found his mind was in a land far removed from Britannia.

On the morning they rounded the southwestern peninsula, the skies cleared and the sun shone through. A day later, the ship halted just off the shoreline. The Norseman decided instead of jumping over the side and getting wet, he would ride atop one of the pallets of supplies being hoisted over the side by a large mechanical crane. Legionaries and sailors alike looked on in amusement. The centurion stood on a pile of tunics and blankets, holding onto the support rope that held the cargo net together.

"Welcome back," said a staff tribune overseeing the offloading of cargo.

Magnus nodded dismissively and made his way into the camp, which had undergone constant improvements to the defences in his absence. It now resembled a semi-permanent fort, complete with watch towers over the gatehouses. As he returned to his tent, he was pleased to see his manservant had kept his kit in immaculate condition. Strapping on his gladius and picking up his vine stick, he decided to seek out General Paulinus or Master Centurion Tyranus. It was Chief Tribune Corbulo he first saw as he stepped into the large principia tent.

"Ah, Centurion Magnus," the young officer said, by way of greeting. "Glad to see you've returned to us."

"It's good to be back, sir," the Norseman acknowledged. "Are Tyranus or the legate around?"

"General Paulinus has not arrived yet. I believe he will be accompanying Governor Scapula on his return in another week or so. The primus pilus is drilling the first cohort on the training stakes today."

The parade field and training stakes had been established just outside the south entrance of the fort. Magnus chuckled, shaking his head as he heard Tyranus' booming voice coming from the drill field.

"Shield boss strikes…go! Come on you lazy, fat bastards! Too much gorging and lack of shit details has made you lot soft!"

The entire cohort was gathered by the stakes. There was enough room for two normal-sized centuries to drill at a time, but only a single double-strength First Cohort century could occupy the stakes at a time. Each legionary was kitted up in full armour, wielding a wicker shield and wooden gladius. With each command they switched their stances and forms of attack. Soldiers punched with their shields, stabbed high and low with their gladii, while attacking with short, rapid chops in the vicinity of where arms and legs would be on an opponent. After a few more minutes, Tyranus blew his whistle. His sweat-soaked legionaries stepped off the field. Every last one of them was red in the face and breathing heavy. Some removed their helmets, running their fingers through wet, matted hair.

"Centurion Furius, the field is yours!"

"Sir!" With a series of sharp commands, Furius' century swarmed the training stakes.

The primus pilus spotted Magnus. "Well, I'll be buggered," he laughed, walking over and extending his hand. "I wasn't sure if you'd be returning. Hell, I half expected to find your request for discharge waiting for my signature."

"No, you have me for a little while longer."

As they clasped hands, Tyranus quickly noticed a change in the Nordic centurion's demeanour and countenance. "Your leave to the old country did you some good, it seems."

"You were more right than you knew, sending me away."

The two walked away from the field. Furius blew his whistle and his legionaries commenced their drills.

"Sure you don't want to oversee your century's drills?" Tyranus asked, looking over his shoulder.

"Caelius can handle it," Magnus replied, shaking his head.

"So who is she?" the master centurion asked, wasting no time.

Magnus grinned broadly.

"A friend of my sister's, if you can believe it. She lost her husband some time ago and has been in a similar emotional state as I have these past four years. Because of Ana, I plan on leaving the legions as soon as we've dealt with Caratacus."

"You realize that may not happen for some time," Tyranus cautioned. "For one thing, most of what we know about his return is little more than rumours. For another, none of us knows what he looks like. It's not like these barbarian kings leave statues of each other like our emperors. And until we can get his army to engage us in a decisive battle, we may never know if we've killed or captured him."

"Yes, a shame our enemies rarely wear uniforms or have busts made of their leaders," Magnus concurred, with a trace of sarcasm. "But, I do understand it may be years before we finish off Caratacus' insurrection. Ana knows this as well. She told me to return to her when I was no longer a soldier of Rome. This does make it a bit more urgent for me that we be done with the Catuvellauni prince. He cannot seem to comprehend that his people have been conquered."

"Do any of these people really understand when they've been subjugated?" Tyranus asked. After a moment he added philosophically, "But then, would you or I?"

Winter's cold embrace crippled Caratacus' spirit. His demeanour had been one of gloom ever since their clash against the Romans. Even Eurgain could not break through her husband's seemingly emotionless wall. His warriors now called the place of the ill-fated ambush 'The Field of Sorrow', in honour of their high king's fallen son.

Perhaps most frustrating was his inability to exact any sort of revenge during the winter months. The Silures had long since dispersed. King Seisyll of Ordovices had made Caratacus his distinguished guest, but there was little his warriors could do before spring.

"I am honoured to have you within my walls," Seisyll emphasised, as he and Caratacus stood atop the barricaded hill that served as the Ordovices capital. "Until such time as you can raise your own stronghold on the ashes of Roman ruins."

145

"Their destruction cannot come soon enough," Caratacus muttered. "They have twenty thousand men encamped along the western shores, yet there is little we can do until they are on the move." He noted the look of concern on Seisyll's face.

"I worry about our supposed allies," the Ordovices king explained. "My people and the Silures have never been on the best of terms. In fact, we have fought more bloody wars against them than any other kingdom in these lands. It is you who brought us together against a common enemy. And I fear King Orin may not be able to control his warriors. Many of them would just as soon put a spear in my guts as they would a Roman."

"The Silures are a proud people," Caratacus said reassuringly, though even he was having doubts as to their commitment to the war against the empire. "They will fight, even if it is in their own way. When I next speak with Orin, I will stress the need for his warriors to continue harrying the imperial army, especially after they have left their winter quarters."

"We will still need more fighters. The Demetae fled the Field of Sorrow without striking a single blow, and I suspect they may be waiting to strike a deal with the Romans. Our protectorates, the Deceangli, learned their lesson after we made an example of their cowardly chief. However, their total number of warriors is very few, no more than four or five thousand."

Caratacus leaned against a tall pillar of the great hall and stared into the distance contemplatively. "We must gather what allies we have while making life a terrible misery for the Romans and those who would prostrate themselves at the feet of Caesar."

Chapter XIV: Valley of Riches

Roman Encampment, near the mouth of the Dyfi River
15 March 49 A.D.

Entrance to an ancient gold mine at Dolaucothi

It was now the Ides of March, that fateful day when Julius Caesar was murdered on the steps of the senate. Governor Scapula and his legates had also returned. A sizeable entourage accompanied Governor Scapula and General Paulinus as they returned to the army's camp. Among them Magnus recognized Queen Cartimandua's courtier, Alaric. But it was the man walking beside the governor and legate that caught the centurion's attention. He was half a head taller than even Paulinus, dressed in an earth coloured toga, with a tartan cloak over his left shoulder. His face was clean shaven, though he had a thick mop of curly black hair atop his head. A wide-bladed broadsword in an ornate scabbard was strapped to his hip.

"Gentlemen, may I present Amminus, son of Cunobeline," Scapula said, introducing the man to his senior officers.

147

"Son of Cunobeline?" Tyranus asked. His eyes widened in realization. "By Victoria, he's Caratacus' brother!"

"An unfortunate circumstance of birth," Amminus said. The corner of his mouth twisted up slightly. His Latin was flawless, and he exuded only a trace of an accent. "I have lived in exile these past eight years. The divine Emperor Claudius has been very kind to me, and his charity has left me with a moral debt to Rome. When I heard my vile brother returned to cause mischief, I felt compelled to offer my services to the empire."

"For starters, you can tell us what your brother looks like," the chief tribune spoke up. "For all we know, he could be dead already."

"No, my brother is anything but dead. You must understand, Caratacus has a viper's tongue that poisons the minds of even great kings. Were he dead, the alliance between the Ordovices and Silures would collapse. They are age-old enemies. That they have named him high king over their own rulers, tells us all we need to know about his powers of persuasion. But worry not, noble tribune, you shall have a detailed description of the serpent. I shall also accompany the governor and will be ready to identify him for your soldiers."

"We depart in three days," Scapula stated. "But before we pursue Caratacus, our newly won friends among the Demetae have promised to show us the way to a 'treasure trove', as they put it."

"I know that of which they speak," Amminus added. "I've never seen it personally but have heard talk, of a vast gold mine on the border of the Demetae and Silures kingdoms. Given the wealth exhibited by King Orin and his ilk, I suspect the rumours may prove true."

Before the trek south could begin, the army had to travel several miles east, in order to find a viable fording point across the River Dyfi. They followed the coast, maintaining a robust advance guard of cavalry, with dispersed cohorts of light auxilia infantry scouring the woods on their flanks. The nimble troopers of these regiments were slowed considerably by the dense woods and undergrowth, the army even more so.

It took the better part of five days to make the fifty mile journey south. Having learned from his mistakes the previous year, Scapula divided his army into three divisions. Legio IX provided the bulwark

148

for the northern column, along with several cohorts of auxilia infantry and one quarter of the cavalry. Legio XX led the centre column, with an equal number of auxilia infantry and cavalry in support. This left half the cavalry and roughly five thousand auxilia infantrymen to make up the southernmost column.

The legionary legates commanded their respective divisions with Governor Scapula accompanying the centre column. Commander Julianus was assigned to lead the auxilia division. They would be skirting the lands of the Demetae, and Scapula needed to ascertain their intentions. Would they offer their spears for Rome, attempt to remain neutral, or were they already under Caratacus' control? The Romans had struggled to tell the various tribes apart, especially during the heat of battle, and could not tell a Demetae from an Ordovices. Only the Silures, with their dark, curly hair and olive skin stood out amongst the various tribes. None of them knew that Demetae warriors had, in fact, been with Caratacus during the last battle, but had balked and fled without taking any part in the fighting.

General Paetus' division skirted a mountain range to the north. Governor Scapula and General Paulinus made their way through a large valley dotted with forests and grass fields. While most of Britannia was lush with vegetation, this was the greenest place Centurion Magnus could recall. He voiced his observation of the land.

"There's some lavender, sir," Optio Caelius pointed out.

"This is ideal grazing country for sheep and cattle," the Norseman added. There were, indeed, scattered groups of sheep and various other animals; however, no people could be seen.

"The people knew we were coming," Magnus remarked.

"They've gone into hiding." his optio concurred.

Due to the openness of the terrain, Paulinus ordered the legion to advance in a series of cohort columns, with the baggage train kept towards the centre, guarded by two cohorts of auxilia infantry. The legion's indigenous cavalry screened the flanks while auxilia horsemen scouted ahead. The governor and legionary command staff rode just behind the First Cohort, accompanied by Amminus. Alaric, who had thus far kept a distance from the exiled Catuvellauni prince, rode with General Paetus. Landon accompanied the auxilia division.

"If my intuition is correct," Amminus said, "we are not far from 'The Valley of Riches'."

"How will we know?" Scapula was sceptical. "It's not as if the Silures have gilded cities or anything remotely resembling civilization."

"I think we'll know when they decide to bid us welcome," Paulinus conjectured.

This drew a knowing grin from Amminus.

"The mines are thought to be little more than a myth to many of the peoples in eastern and northern Britannia. The torques of gold worn by many of their warriors tell me it is no fable. The Silures may not be as well armed as your soldiers; however, one is much more likely to see swords and mail armour among them than any other tribe."

Scapula pondered this for a moment then gave his assessment. "If they weren't such an unorganized rabble, they could be a rich and powerful adversary."

"They are already powerful," Paulinus remarked. "But I agree, we should be thankful they haven't used their potential wealth to field a well-equipped, professional army."

"Some say the gold is cursed," Amminus added. "This is nonsense. It is a matter of the mines being in close proximity to both Silures and Demetae lands. These hills and valleys have been the grave of many warriors who died trying to claim the treasures as their own."

"My king, the Romans are near Dolaucothi," a scout reported to King Orin.

While this caused much consternation amongst the elders and chief warriors, it was the opportunity he had been waiting for. His warlords had been in such constant dispute as to how to deal with the invaders, that it left him unable to marshal a sizeable force. If he could not control his own warriors, what hope was there to maintain the alliance with the Ordovices under Caratacus?

"Does their entire army approach?" he asked.

"No," the man said, shaking his head. "We saw but one eagle standard and only a few thousand other troops."

"Meaning they've divided their forces," one of the elders noted.

Orin nodded. "They've learned their lessons from the previous year. Send scouts to find the remainder of their fighters. If one legion approaches the Valley of Riches, the rest cannot be far away."

While glad for a chance to spill copious amounts of Roman blood, the king was feeling the constrictions of both time and distance. With his warriors still scattered to their homes and the imperial army fast approaching the precious mines, there was not enough time to rally his entire army to face them. Caratacus would have to be informed at once, though his army with King Seisyll was even further afield than the majority of the Silures warriors.

"Muster every fighter within twenty miles," he ordered. "The mines must not fall into Roman hands!"

The Silures had been given a brief, unexpected reprieve, as Paulinus' division unwittingly encamped only five miles from the mines. Had they known how close they were, and that the valley was only modestly defended, they may have launched their assault right away. As it was, the thick woods impeded their reconnaissance cavalry from scouting too far ahead. It was only when the late afternoon sun began to slowly dip into the west that reports came back, informing them the legendary mines were found.

"Well, bugger it," Paulinus sighed with mild frustration. "We could have slaughtered the bastards and camped there tonight."

"I left several of my men to keep an eye on the complex," the scout section leader reported. "There was a lot of activity within. It appears they are mustering warriors from all over the region."

"Which means they know we're here," Scapula muttered.

"We need to deploy pickets well ahead of the army," Paulinus recommended. "Otherwise, these bastards may have a slew of surprises waiting for us."

"I have to agree, General," Amminus concurred. "The Silures are known for laying traps and ambushes. They will likely try to soften up your forces before they reach the mines."

The scout had taken a long stick and drawn a crude sketch in the dirt. "It is a large complex, sirs," he said. "There are plenty of stockades for slaves near the mine shafts, with what can best be described as a barracks for guards."

"How many guards?" General Paulinus asked.

"It's hard to say, sir. We got as close as we could, but they have pickets posted well beyond the compound. The woods on the surrounding hills are very thick. I would hazard several hundred warriors, at least, though they could soon be reinforced by an entire army."

"I cannot see Caratacus leaving this place undefended," Amminus remarked. "Even if he felt it unimportant, there is no way King Orin would let his greatest source of wealth fall into our hands without a fight."

"A pity we didn't bring any artillery," Scapula grumbled.

"Do you want to drag onagers and ammunition wagons through this shit?" Paulinus countered. "We'd still be fifty miles from here if we'd tried bringing them with us."

"Enough," Scapula interrupted with irritation. He'd grown tired of his legates constantly undermining him, when they weren't squabbling with each other. What troubled him more was that despite his age and position as governor-general of the province, he possessed neither the innate skill nor battle experience of either Paetus or Paulinus. He was compelled to rely on both men, and as often as not, their ideas for dealing with the insurrection varied greatly.

"Whether we should have brought the siege trains with us or not is irrelevant," he said forcefully. He broke into a coughing fit, quietly cursing his lungs for still bothering him, even after taking time to convalesce during the winter months. He took a deep breath and continued, "We will simply have to overwhelm them with what forces we have available."

It would prove to be a long night for both Romans and Silures. Paulinus ordered the auxilia infantry cohorts to post the picket outposts in the woods leading to the mines, with the cavalry kept in ready reserve. This upset many of the commanders as well as their troopers. They perceived the legion as being left safe within its fortified camp, while they battled the 'night demons of these woods'. Scapula had berated the men, telling them to follow orders, while Paulinus made it known that Legio XX would be handling the brunt of the assault in the morning. No one slept that night, as the cries of men and sounds of skirmishing echoed throughout the forests and across the valley. It was a confusing frenzy. In the utter blackness of the thick woods, it was impossible to tell friend from foe.

"Must be hell for those poor bastards," Centurion Furius said as he joined Magnus near the eastern ramparts.

It was nearly midnight.

"They're doing their job whether they realize it or not," Magnus observed. "Hopefully, we won't have too many surprises waiting for us in the morning."

Dawn came at last. While decani conducted final inspections of their men, General Paulinus called a meeting of all cohort commanders and First Cohort centurions.

"I've received word from the auxilia cohort commanders," the legate said. "A lot of their boys took a beating last night."

"How bad was it, sir?" Tyranus asked.

"Some of them didn't get hit at all. Other groups were almost completely annihilated. It's still fairly dark in the woods. But, I imagine they gave as well as they took. No doubt the Silures did not expect us to have troops waiting for them out there. A pity we didn't have time to set proper counter-ambushes." His voice was filled with regret. The auxiliaries were not his men, but they were still soldiers of Rome and had died in service to the empire.

"We're sending cavalry to the hills north and south of the complex," Paulinus continued. "Cohorts Seven and Eight will swing wide to the left, approaching from the northwest. Cohorts Nine and Ten will attack from the south and southwest. The rest of the legion will conduct a broad assault straight up the centre."

"We'll be passing the auxilia pickets," Tyranus noted, "So be sure to let the auxiliaries know you're friendly forces. There won't be any subtleties about this attack. The Silures know we're coming."

After answering a few more questions, Paulinus dismissed his commanders back to their units. Magnus made his way back to the First Cohort's Third Century to where Optio Caelius and the tesserarius were finishing up the inspection of their legionaries.

153

"What are the orders, sir?" Caelius asked.

Magnus replied with a question of his own. "Are we ready to pound these fucks into oblivion?"

"That we are, sir."

"Then let's go give these bastards a Roman-style thrashing!"

Magnus' last words elicited a loud ovation from his men. They were inspired by this newly found energy and aggression coming from their centurion. Indeed, Magnus felt as if he were ten years younger. He was filled with the burning anticipation of battle that had been dormant within him for far too long.

The cornicens sounded the call to arms. General Paulinus and the staff tribunes rode to where the aquilifer stood with the eagle standard held high.

"Twentieth Legion!" the legate shouted, raising his spatha. *"To the eagle!"*

Wordlessly, nearly five thousand imperial legionaries rushed to their place on the massive battle line. The designated wing cohorts followed a handful of guides from the legion's indigenous cavalry. The main assault force dressed their ranks and made ready to advance. Once all cohorts were in position, the eagle was raised up and then dipped forward, signalling the advance. Eyes were wide as they proceeded through the dense woods. It was a slow and somewhat awkward trek. Soldiers stepped on or tripped over fallen logs, with javelins, shields, and helmets snagging low hanging branches and undergrowth.

It was only an hour after dawn. The sun's rays had yet to fully illuminate the darkness. Because of their impeded vision, officers were ordered to call out the watchword of *'Germanicus'* to alert the battered and exhausted auxiliaries who'd been through a hellish night. Centurion Magnus would see just how harrowing their ordeal was when he called out the watchword.

"Britannicus! Britannicus!" A near-panicked voice shouted from less than thirty feet away.

Magnus pulled a large thicket aside to see the battered remains of a twenty-man picket crouching together behind their shields. Seven of their number were dead, covered in blood with their entrails split open. Two were missing arms. A third slain trooper had his lower leg severed. Almost all who survived were covered in injuries. The decanus in command had his right arm in a makeshift

154

sling made from shreds of a cloak. His face was covered in blood and filth, like most of his men, and his eyes were wide with terror, exhaustion, and now relief. Around their position lay nearly a score of Silures corpses. Those wounded and not saved by their companions had had their throats cut by the maddened auxiliaries.

"We thought you lot abandoned us," the section leader said, through gritted teeth.

"Withdraw back to camp," Magnus replied.

He and his men did not cease in their tramp through the woods. While he pitied the troopers and understood better than most what they had been through, they could not stop the advance to assist them.

"Poor bastards," his signifier muttered. His eyes locked with those of the auxilia decanus. The signum then caught on a branch, causing the signifier to break into a fit of profanity as he wrenched the standard free.

There were similar grim discoveries made all along the legion's frontage. A couple of pickets had been overrun completely, with only a handful of badly wounded survivors found amid the bodies. And despite their terrible sacrifice, they had failed to completely prevent the Silures from laying a series of traps and ambushes. Magnus and his soldiers could hear the sound of shouts and war cries echoing through the woods.

"Look alive, lads," he said, drawing his gladius and hefting his shield. His timing proved fortuitous. A sling stone that should have smashed into his face instead bounced off his shield. *"Down!"*

A volley of throwing darts and sling bullets flew from a previously unseen defilade directly in front of them. His entire century quickly dropped to their knees, shields in the second to sixth ranks raised up to provide overhead protection. The barbarian salvo proved mostly ineffective, as the trees and brush that gave concealment also impeded many of their missiles from striking home.

"Century...up!"

Magnus' legionaries were burning with anger. They pressed onward. As they forced their way through another thicket patch, the ground suddenly sloped downward about fifteen feet. Legionaries stumbled down through the ankle high grasses, reaching a path below. Directly to their front was a nearly impassable wall of ferns and sticker bushes.

"Oh, fuck me!" a legionary snapped. He tried to crash through with his full weight behind his shield.

"There's nothing for it, we'll have to go around," Magnus admitted begrudgingly.

There were many such obstacles that broke up the formations of the Twentieth Legion. This gave the Silures the chance to bombard them further, while launching harassing attacks on the extreme flanks.

"This way, sir!" a decanus on the extreme left shouted.

The Norseman ordered his men to follow the sergeant around the mass of ferns and thickets, to where the valley opened up into a series of small, grass covered hills. At one point they almost crashed into the First Century. Master Centurion Tyranus was leading them out of a similarly thick stand of woods.

"Bugger me, but it is a fucking mess back there!" the primus pilus said. He laughed in defiance but with a trace of nervousness.

"At least we've found their compound," Magnus remarked, nodding his head towards the large networks of huts and forges that dotted the hills.

"Let's go claim it for the emperor!"

As various cohorts smashed their way out of the woods, General Paulinus was spotted off to their right, attempting to reform the legion into a more coherent assault force.

"Glad to see you still with us, sir," Tyranus said, as the legate rode up to them.

"The flank cohorts on the right are in a nasty scrap," Paulinus informed him. "I've sent Corbulo to ascertain the situation on the left. How goes it here?"

"Once we get everyone out of these damned woods, we'll be ready to assault the stronghold," Tyranus informed him.

Down below, they could see hundreds of Silures fighters fleeing for the perceived safety of their barricades. Their mates stood behind the crude stockades, shields and spears ready for battle. As a sign of Silures wealth, nearly half wore mail shirts belted in the middle. Though lacking the additional shoulder guards worn by Roman auxiliaries, it was still a sign of status that so many of their fighters had some form of protection.

"Let's break these bastards," Magnus growled.

With the blow of his whistle, the century began its methodical jog towards the defences. Enemy skirmishers continued to pelt them with the occasional missile weapon, but there was no stopping the ferocious onslaught of the Twentieth Legion. At less than thirty feet from the growing mass of enemy warriors, the Romans unleashed their own form of hell.

"Front rank...throw!"

Hundreds of javelins sailed over the Silures' makeshift barricades, impaling many a warrior and smashing through the shields of those who managed to raise them in time.

"Second rank...throw!"

With the unleashing of a second storm of death, the Silures instinctively withdrew into the compound.

Magnus and the other centurions ordered their men to use controlled volleys with the rest of the javelins, keeping the defenders at bay, while the first two ranks assailed the stockade. Legionaries hacked through the ropes holding the stakes and sharpened poles together, creating a series of breaches in a matter of minutes.

Grinning sinisterly, Magnus looked over his shoulder and pointed his gladius to the nearest gap in the crumbling barricade. *"With me, lads!"* With a shout of rage, the entire Third Century swarmed into the compound, the wreckage of the stockade only breaking up their formations momentarily. As the Romans stepped on and over the fallen barbarians, the remaining Silures warriors found their courage and charged into the wall of shields and flashing blades. The Norseman rammed one assailant, heaving all of his weight behind his shield. The crash left the Silures fighter off balance, giving Magnus just enough time to plunge his gladius into the man's guts. Though wearing a mail shirt that may have offered some protection against a barbarian spear, it proved useless against a heavy, sharpened imperial sword with a powerful Norseman behind it. The rings of the mail burst, and Magnus' weapon plunged deep into the warrior's guts. The stricken man howled in agony as blood spurted onto Magnus' hand.

As more and more imperial soldiers stormed into the compound, the Silures warriors found themselves outnumbered and outmatched. If King Orin had had a week or better to muster his people, perhaps they could have made a viable stand against the Romans. Given the hellish terrain the legion had to make its way through just to reach the mines, they could have set a sizeable ambush and succeeded where Caratacus had failed. As it was, men were falling, attempting in vain to break the legionary shield wall. And while fiercely brave, the Silures were also pragmatists. There would be another time to fight the Romans, and they could always reclaim their gold another day. Within twenty minutes of the Twentieth Legion storming the barricades, the deep bellow of a war horn sounded the order for the Silures to retreat.

"They win this one," a war chief muttered.

Chapter XV: To Tame a Land

***

The rugged terrain and dense woods prevented Paulinus' division from completely surrounding the mines at Dolaucothi. And since the actual clash of arms was disappointingly short lived, only a few dozen Silures warriors lay dead or wounded; scarcely sufficient retribution for the Romans' losses this day.

Magnus slowly calmed down from his rush of fury. He breathed a sigh of relief when he saw his own century had escaped mostly unscathed. There were but a handful of wounded, and these were mostly minor injuries to the arms and legs.

"It's just a flesh wound," one legionary said dismissively, despite the copious amounts of blood that had run down his arm.

Off to the far left of the compound, Centurion Metellus and the Fifth Cohort found the prisoner stockades; large, uncovered enclaves filled with hundreds of men. All were young, for one did not grow old working in the mines. Many had vacant, distant eyes. Others clutched the bars of their prison, staring in wonder at the armoured soldiers who had driven off their hated overlords.

"Secure this compound," Metellus ordered one of his centurions. "I don't want this lot running off."

Governor Scapula and General Paulinus rode over to the centurion, who saluted them. They were joined by Amminus and Landon, who quickly dismounted and rushed over to the stockades.

"Looking for old friends, is he?" Scapula asked.

"Silures and Brigantes have been at war since anyone can remember," Amminus explained. "I have no doubt there are Brigantes amongst these prisoners."

His assumptions were confirmed when Landon started speaking feverishly with a young man who sat next to the barricade, his head slumped in his lap. Landon pleaded with the man, reaching through the bars to grasp his filthy hand.

"Who is he?" Paulinus asked, kneeling next to the Brigantes man.

"An old friend. We served together as part of the queen's guard. He disappeared, along with many of our friends, following a Silures raid soon after the war ended." He looked to the legate, eyes wet with tears. "I doubt we'll find many more still alive, but I must look for any of my countrymen who may be imprisoned here."

Paulinus nodded and turned back to Scapula. "The Brigantes are among our most important allies. We should free any we find and return them to Queen Cartimandua."

"Very well," the governor replied. "It will be the emperor's gift for her continued loyalty."

"What of the rest?" Landon asked.

"What of them?" Scapula countered. "We need slaves to work these mines. Any man here who is not from Brigantes will remain."

Landon looked at Paulinus.

"Everyone in this land own slaves, to include your own people," the legate chastised. "These mines are of no use to us without a labour force."

It was a harsh but accurate assessment.

Landon knew it was hypocritical for him to condemn the Romans for leaving most of the prisoners as slaves. After all, there were many a Silures captive who toiled until death in the Brigantes' mines and stone quarries. The governor and legate left Centurion Metellus and his cohort to assist Landon in sorting his countrymen from the other prisoners. Doubtless there would be those who would claim to be from Brigantes, once they realized those men would be set free. Regardless, Scapula was still pleased to have claimed this prize for the emperor.

"Now to see the mines themselves," he said. He kicked his horse into a trot and led his entourage to where he heard the shafts were located.

The main shaft itself was rather underwhelming. It was little more than a large tunnel in the side of a hill. Legionaries stood guard at the entrance. Others ignited torches and made ready to sweep the tunnel of any Silures fighters who might be hiding within. Centurion Furius and his century from the First Cohort were preparing to conduct the search.

"Not much to look at," the centurion primus ordo remarked. "But, these barbarians are not very adept at harvesting resources."

Scapula nodded and added, "If there is even a fraction of the gold we are led to believe, then we shall make this a source of wealth for both the province and empire."

"About that, governor," Paulinus said quietly, into Scapula's ear. He tipped his head away from the crowd of soldiers and other officers.

The governor was irritated by the doubting tone in the legate's voice and made certain he knew it. "Already having doubts about our victory?" he asked in exasperation.

"Not at all," Paulinus replied. "We have captured what could potentially be a great source of wealth for the empire. My question is, how do you intend to keep it?" He paused for an answer.

Scapula stared at him, his brow creased in confusion.

The legate sighed and continued, "Governor, we are in the midst of an entirely hostile land at least two day's trek from the coast. We don't know the intentions of the Demetae. Some of them have come to us professing to be friends, but not their rulers. We can only hope they have not been poisoned by Caratacus' serpent tongue. The rest of this land is entirely owned by the Silures."

"Piss on them," Scapula spat. "Cowardly bastards ran like a bunch of frightened old women. They have no stomach for a fight against Rome."

"If you were to ask any of our veterans who were in the invasion, they would tell you a different tale," Paulinus countered. "The Silures are anything but cowardly. They didn't make a more defiant stand because they did not have the numbers. Don't think for a moment they will allow us to keep this crown of their wealth."

"What would you have me do, then?" Scapula was clearly frustrated.

"We should take the time to build a proper fort," he recommended. "One that will house at least three cohorts of infantry, plus cavalry detachments."

"It will take at least a month to build a proper fort," the governor complained, "even with the entire Twentieth Legion here. I'll have to send word to the other divisions so they can halt their advance."

"Would you rather we lose the emperor's prize before he's seen a single piece of its gold?" Paulinus countered. "Besides, leaving a sizeable garrison here will draw many Silures away from supporting Caratacus."

Scapula smirked at this assessment. "Of course. It will drive those bastards out of their filthy minds knowing we sit on their riches, with no way to get them back. Very well, we'll take whatever time we need to fortify this position; even if we cannot claim its wealth for some time. We'll detach three auxilia infantry cohorts to garrison the fort, plus a single company of cavalry. They only need enough horsemen to provide reconnaissance."

"That should be sufficient," Paulinus agreed. "I'll have the legion begin harvesting timber and digging fortifications as soon as possible."

With no small measure of difficulty, Scapula managed to get messages to his other divisions, informing them of the delay. While neither General Paetus nor Commander Julianus was happy to halt their march across the Silures Kingdom, the idea of claiming a large gold mine for the empire was too great an opportunity to squander.

It was with an added measure of relief when the Julianus arrived at the centre column's camp, accompanied by the chief of the Demetae. Scapula had a dais erected near the site of the fort's principia. Pillars bearing busts of the emperor and the gods, Jupiter, Mars, Victoria, and Bellona, were placed on the four corners; the additional statues having been brought with the legate's baggage, following his spring return. All the standards, including Legio XX's eagle, were placed behind the governor's chair. General Paulinus and Commander Julianus were given seats on either side of the governor. The legion's chief and staff tribunes stood behind the three. All had their armour polished and their best traveling cloaks draped over the left shoulder. A guard of honour from the First Cohort lined the path leading to the principia. All cohort commanders and centurions primus ordo gathered at the base of the dais.

The Demetae chieftain strode boldly towards Scapula with a small entourage of nobles. Landon walked beside him, acting as interpreter. The chieftain was of average height, with reddish hair pulled back in a ponytail, and a luxuriant thick moustache neatly combed off either end of his lip. He stood bare-chested with a green cloak draped over his shoulders. A large broadsword hung from his left hip. His head was adorned with a bronze circlet. He said a few words and bowed with his hand extended.

"Chief Judoc of the Demetae bids us welcome to his lands," Landon translated for Scapula. "He thanks you for liberating his mines from the malevolent Silures."

"Tell him I appreciate his sentiments," the governor replied. "However, these mines now belong to the Emperor of Rome."

As Landon translated, Scapula kept his gaze fixed on Judoc, whose face remained impassive. The governor thought the Demetae chieftain would take offence to his assertion that the mines were no longer theirs.

His expression remained emotionless. Judoc simply nodded and said a few calm words of acceptance.

"He says he understands why Caesar would claim the mines as his own. However, he also states, Caesar will need friends in the region if he is to keep them from the Silures."

Scapula looked to Paulinus, who gave a barely perceptible nod. It surprised the legate that the governor was seeking his implicit approval.

"I am certain we can come to some sort of arrangement," he said, in a very measured tone. "But for now, tell the chief that he and his nobles are my guests, and Caesar welcomes them in friendship as allies of Rome."

It was very presumptive of Scapula. Judoc had made no mention of forging an alliance with the empire; however, he knew that diplomatically, he'd made it difficult for the Demetae to presume otherwise. After all, though his terms were vague, Chief Judoc could assume he would be entitled to at least a portion of the gold mined in return for his allegiance to Rome. Even a paltry sum would be better than when the Silures controlled Dolaucothi. The imperial army would remain static for some time while they built up and fortified the area, so there would be opportunities for the Demetae to make the most of this proposed alliance. The high king, Caratacus, and King Orin of Silures would be incensed by this. But as long as they were distracted fighting the Romans, Judoc reckoned he had little to fear. Even if the Silures did seek retribution, the Demetae warriors would fare far better against them than against the massive horde of Caesar's armoured soldiers.

For the high king, the Demetae were not a concern. At least, not one Caratacus wished to deal with at the time. He had just learned of the Roman attack on Dolaucothi and knew nothing of Chief Judoc's submission to Caesar. Instead, his focus was on breaking the will of their potentially greatest ally who, thus far, had been kept in check by their weak-willed and feckless queen. If he could not gain the allegiance of the most powerful kingdom in the midlands of Britannia, then he would make them bleed for surrendering to the invaders.

On this night, they would not be doing a simple raid of a Brigantes farming community. Instead, the high king would make a profound statement by destroying the small occupying force Queen Cartimandua had posted near the River Dyfi. With Venutius covertly causing discontent in the northern and eastern regions of the kingdom, the queen had been unable to reinforce the Dyfi garrison with additional troops. She had petitioned the Roman government for assistance, but the governor was fighting his campaign against the Silures, and the rest of their forces were stretched thin across the province. As such, his deputies at Camulodunum were hesitant to dispatch imperial soldiers without his permission.

Two thousand Ordovices warriors accompanied the high king, with several hundred fighters dispatched by King Orin of Silures. The Brigantes defence works were only a fort in the loosest sense of the word. With a wooden palisade atop minimal earthworks, it paled in comparison to the strongholds built by Caratacus' allies or by their hated Roman adversaries. There was also a small village less than a mile away. The high king promised to give it as spoils to his warriors once they were victorious.

Torches were tied to long poles near the rickety gate. A smattering of others could be seen being carried by occasional sentries atop the earthworks.

Fear grips them, Caratacus thought to himself, smiling sinisterly. The full moon caused his crouching warriors to cast a plethora of dancing shadows, like spirits of death waiting to strike. They kept low, hoping to avoid being spotted by the enemy sentries until the last possible moment. When they were within thirty feet of the gate, the high king stood and drew his broadsword. He took a deep breath, and wordlessly began to run towards the unfortunate souls who stood half asleep just outside the gate. *Poor fools, if you'd only remained behind your walls, you may have lived a few minutes longer.*

Scores of warriors rushed beside and behind Caratacus, weapons ready to strike. The sleepy-eyed guard had only a second to realize the horror of what was happening, before the high king's heavy blade cleaved his head from his shoulders. The man's companion cried out in pain, as several spears were plunged into his body. Caratacus watched gleefully as the twitching corpse of his first victim fell thrashing to the ground, gouts of blood gushing from the stump where his head had once been.

A startled shout came from the defences. The attackers saw numerous torches flickering, as their bearers rushed to sound the alarm. Caratacus nodded to one of his men, who carried a war horn. The ominous blaring alerted the sleeping garrison and signalled for the assault to commence in earnest.

Ordovices fighters shouted oaths and war cries as they assailed the ramparts of the small fort. To their credit, the venerable Brigantes warriors were quick to rouse themselves and arm for battle. Two of Caratacus' more nimble men had just enough time to be hoisted over the palisade and open the gate, before they were swarmed by their enemies, who quickly cut them down. The high king quietly promised to make an offering to Aeron after the battle, in tribute to their selfless sacrifice. With a shout of rage, he and his men stormed into the fort.

Brigantes men were scrambling to repel the overwhelming waves of attackers. Spears were plunged into numerous warriors who had not been quick enough in scrambling over the palisades, yet the resistance proved futile. Dozens of assailants exploited numerous gaps in the earthworks that were devoid of defenders. Caratacus led the charge through the gate with scores of warriors following. The situation quickly became hopeless for the Brigantes.

The high king brought his sword down with a mighty smash, breaking the skull of one hapless defender who immediately slumped to the ground. Blood, brain, and bits of bone protruded through his split scalp. His warriors overwhelmed the man's companions with stabs of the spear, and the chopping of sword and axe.

165

Caratacus loathed Queen Cartimandua, but had to admire the tenacity with which her warriors fought. He hoped, one day, to call them allies. It was a shame these men would never know Caratacus as a friend. Every last one would die this night. Sword and spear sunk into flesh, shattered bone, and disembowelled the stricken in a cacophony of horror. Soon the ground was soaked in blood, made slippery in places by piles of viscera. Their huts were then set alight, while many were trapped inside and left to be slowly burned to death. The Brigantes fought valiantly, leaving many of Caratacus' warriors dead or severely maimed. Yet, in the end, their numbers were simply too few. In less than an hour, there was not a single Brigantes warrior alive within the fort.

Caratacus stood atop the ramparts. The burning huts of the fort seemed to make him glow with an aura that mirrored his rage. He held the head of the guard he decapitated in one hand, still wielding his bloodied broadsword in the other. He raised both high, eliciting howls of triumph from his men.

"Now, my friends, the village is yours as promised! Take what you will, and kill anyone you find!"

The light from the fires alerted the few souls still awake at this late hour, and they quickly sounded the alarm within the village. Some of the men armed themselves to fight. Others fled into the woods with their families. Perhaps half of the citizens managed to escape before Caratacus' warriors were unleashed in all their fury. There would be more blood spilled, with the women raped before they were murderously butchered.

Though barbaric, Caratacus' methods differed very little from his Roman adversaries. Like them, he had attempted to use diplomacy to win over the Brigantes long before he resorted to brutal force. And, like the Romans, he was not afraid to use terror as the ultimate weapon of persuasion. The carnage that greeted Queen Cartimandua and the nobles of her court a few days later sickened them. Many were filled with fear, as Caratacus had hoped. The queen, however, would prove a very difficult foe to break.

It would be midsummer by the time Paulinus' division finished with the fort at Dolaucothi. He'd been surprisingly generous to the

Demetae, wishing to keep the pressure off the garrison he would be leaving behind while securing the rear of his army from attack. Chief Judoc asked that he be aided in acquiring some of the lands near the western Silures border, and his people be given a measure of independence under Rome. In return, his warriors would assist the war effort by launching raids into Silures lands, to include the acquisition of slaves to work the mines.

"They seem anxious to become our friends," Scapula said to Paulinus as they dined one evening.

"Their chief has seen our soldiers," the legate observed. "Every last one of our men is better armoured and equipped than even Judoc himself. I doubt his demeanour is as friendly as he tries to make it; however, he was wise enough to know the alternative to becoming our ally was facing annihilation."

"You never cease to amaze me, General," Scapula remarked. "You advise me to be diplomatic and civil to these barbarians, and yet, you do not hesitate to threaten them with extermination."

"If one method of diplomacy fails, then we must be ready to use another," Paulinus replied with cold detachment. "I may only be the legate of a legion, but if I ever intend to sit in your chair then I'd better learn to use every form of persuasion available. I must say, being posted to a very new, and mostly untamed province has been a far better tutor than I could have imagined."

"You are midway through your three-year tour with the legion," Scapula observed. "And yet, I suspect that after you leave, Britannia will not have seen the last of you."

The days of waiting for the fort to be completed became an irritating grind to the governor. Despite the exceptionally large labour force available, a substantial number of his soldiers were required for security and conducting constant patrols of the region. The fort itself was large enough to house nearly two thousand imperial soldiers. There were three rows of deep trenches, lined with obstacles, dug around its ramparts. The woods within a half mile of the fort were completely deforested to provide fields of observation as well as timber for the walls, guard towers, and other structures. A large structure was built to serve as headquarters for the garrison commander, a senior ranking auxilia centurion. The soldiers would continue to live out of tents for the time being. Though they were making every effort to fortify the stronghold, Scapula was not entirely certain whether this was a temporary or permanent incursion into Silures territory. But for now, security was of greater importance than soldier comfort.

"Looks like we won't be catching Caratacus this year after all," Tyranus said.

He and Magnus observed the handiwork of their legionaries.

"Maybe not," the Norseman reluctantly concurred. "Though I do believe having a Roman garrison in the middle of his united kingdoms is a grave insult. It may be just the motivation he needs to finally face us in open battle."

There was little for the centre column except tedium on long march back to Roman territory, during what remained of the campaign season. While capturing the gold mine at Dolaucothi had been a substantial prize for the empire, securing it had cost them any chance of capturing Caratacus or engaging his army in a decisive engagement. And, it would be some time before they could make use of the mines. Though they secured an alliance with the Demetae, Governor Scapula was beginning to understand that the wealth of Dolaucothi could never be fully exploited, so long as the Silures remained a threat in the region.

Word soon reached the governor regarding the horrific attack upon the Brigantes border fort and the nearby village. Though Cartimandua was as stalwart of an ally as ever, the royal court was becoming even more divided as to who they should align themselves with. Despite the atrocities committed against their people, there were growing numbers who would have Brigantes break their alliance with Rome and join with Caratacus. For both sides, patience was running thin. As the army retired across the River Sabrina, Scapula and his legates knew the following year would see an end to the war against Caratacus, one way or the other.

Chapter XVI: Here We Will Stand

Near Caer Caradoc, west of the River Sabrina
November 49 A.D.
***

Autumn had come once more to Britannia. The previous campaign season was one of modest victories and great frustrations for both sides. For Caratacus, the death of his son took an immeasurable toll upon his spirit. The loss of the gold mine at Dolaucothi had been a source of great consternation for the Silures, who were now embroiled in a renewed conflict with the Demetae. Yet the Romans could scarcely claim victory. They may have captured the mines, but as long as the region was in a state of war they could make no use of them. They had committed numerous soldiers and resources just trying to keep the mine from falling back into Silures hands.

With the imperial army retired across the Sabrina, Caratacus knew it was time to prepare for the decisive battle against Rome that the people so craved. In the forested hills where the River Sabrina ambled westward, the high king met with the erstwhile high druid, Tathal. Here was a sacred shrine, though it only consisted of a natural stone altar in a small meadow surrounded by tall trees.

Caratacus knelt before the shrine. Buried deep within a nearly impassable forest, few even knew of its existence. They were just twelve miles from the Sabrina, and the far banks, his scouts had told him, were swarming with imperial soldiers. Thus far, they appeared content to fortify their encampments, waiting to see where Caratacus and his allies would appear again.

His greatest difficulty was keeping his army fed during the winter months. Unlike their Roman adversaries, none of the tribesmen had any real concept of logistics. The high king had sent over half his warriors home to tend to their crops, with the pledge they would bring a portion of the harvest to his encampment and return to fight in the spring. However, as most of the Silures were committed to their war against the Demetae, King Orin could only promise five thousand men from his elite guard, even after the frost was off the ground.

Only Seisyll and Orin accompanied him this day to the shrine. Tathal and a half-score of druids he had never seen before awaited them. Caratacus was filled with uncertainty. He needed to know if the gods favoured them in this war against the invaders.

"We bid you welcome, Caratacus, High King of Britannia," Tathal said respectfully. "You come seeking the favour of the gods."

"I do," Caratacus replied. His face was hard. Before Tathal could speak further, he said, "And I do not want to hear any talk of additional sacrifice. The gods have already taken my son. If that does not appease them, then they can rot in the abyss of oblivion."

"Calm yourself, friend," Tathal said, holding up one hand. "If one wishes favour from the gods, it is not wise to blaspheme. Aeron is pleased with you. You have soaked the earth in the blood of traitors."

"You mean the Brigantes?"

Tathal nodded. "They will come to you in due time, my friend. Cartimandua's hold upon her people is weak. Yet you have come here not to fight against the defilers from Brigantes, but the invaders from the unholy empire."

"The ground here is good," Caratacus stated. "My men can build a great stronghold here."

The druid closed his eyes in thought and seemed to fall into a trance for a few moments. Finally he said, "This place is called Caer Caradoc. Trust in the gods, and you will find victory."

Three temporary legionary forces now bordered the hostile lands of westernmost Britannia. Scapula ordered Legio II, Augusta, to occupy just north of the vast southern bay of the River Sabrina. Sixty miles to the north, following the river, Legio IX, Hispania established its quarters for the coming winter. Twenty miles further, where the river turned to the west, was the camp of Legio XX, Valeria. Of all the legionary forces in Britannia, only Legio XIV, Gemina Martia Victrix, remained at the capital fortress of Camulodunum.

"Let us hope the rest of the province remains docile," Magnus said. He stood near the bank of the river, his cloak wrapped around him.

The Sabrina forked around a large, tree covered island that extended a few hundred meters from end-to-end. Just north, the river began its meandering course to the west.

"I heard the Cornovii king has petitioned Scapula with establishing a permanent fortress here," Tyranus remarked. "Apparently auxiliaries and their own warriors aren't enough to save them from the terrors that lurk across the river."

Magnus snorted at the master centurion's contemptuous assessment. "It seems almost every tribe strong enough to stand on their own wants to pick a fight with Rome. The rest cower beneath our tunic skirts. Ah well, I say let the Fourteenth have this place, and the rest of us can go home."

"After we've finished with Caratacus."

"Do you think he finally intends to fight us?" the Norseman asked.

"According to his brother." Tyranus shrugged. "I have no idea how he gathers his intelligence, and I'm not sure I want to."

"His methods are likely no worse than ours," Magnus remarked. "And if what he says is true, then Caratacus plans to make a stand against us not far from this very spot."

"Centurion Magnus," a voice said, behind them.

Both men turned to see a young legionary, likely an aid to the command staff.

The soldier saluted the two senior officers before continuing. "Beg your pardon, sir, but a message came through the imperial post addressed directly to you." He handed the thick, weathered scroll to the primus ordo before saluting once more and taking his leave.

"Someone sending you love letters?" Tyranus asked, grinning.

Magnus broke open the worn seal and began to read. "It's from my brother-in-law," he said.

"Valens?"

The Norseman silently read through the first few lines. It was dated from several months before. Valens would've had to wait for a merchant vessel from the empire to reach the northlands, before he could send it on. As he read, Magnus' face started to turn a slight shade of red, his eyes misting slightly.

Tyranus thought the news must be terrible, until Magnus' face broke into the broadest smile the master centurion reckoned he had ever seen. "Well, what is it? Do tell!"

171

"I'm a father…"

Magnus, you magnificent bastard!

Let me be the first to congratulate you on giving Svetlana and I a strapping young nephew. Granted, Ana did almost all the work. She had to carry the little bastard for nine months, after you popped off back to Britannia. Not to worry, she is doing well. It would take more than the spawn of your seed to break a woman of her fortitude. Ana was uncertain as to a name. But, since his father is a Roman, she thought it only fitting to give the lad a Roman name. I suggested Titus Flavianus Spurius and did not think you would object.

Magnus smiled as he read the name. It was fitting that his son would share the given name of his lifelong friend, Titus Artorius Justus. He continued to read:

It would seem young Titus has made Ana realize what is important in life. She told me she now understands that 'home' is not so much a place, but the people in one's life…at least I think it was something to that effect. You know how bloody sentimental women can be. She also said, rather forcefully I might add, that her son needed his father. It will likely be next spring before Ana is fit to travel, which will give her plenty of time to sort all her affairs here before she comes chasing after you.

I hope that Mars, Odin, or whatever damned gods may actually exist, will grant our armies victory over Caratacus. I further hope that when it's over, your own soul will at last find peace. So do us all a favour, and don't be getting yourself killed between now and then. And after you finally decide it's time to leave the life of the legions behind, no dying of old age before young Titus can make you a grandfather! Oh, and your sister sends her love. Fight well, my friend, but know that there is a life worth having outside of the legions.

Your brother,

"Ever more reason to not allow Caratacus to spill your guts, old friend," Tyranus said, with a friendly slap on the shoulder.

Magnus grunted in reply, took a deep breath, and tried to take in what had happened. He'd given up any hope of children since Achillia's death, and it was utterly surreal that he now had a son. He then decided, no matter what happened this coming campaign season, he was finished with the legions. The old centurion knew he'd stayed in the ranks far too long. He would help his legion attempt to settle its score with Caratacus and move on.

He returned to his tent and began to write a reply letter to Valens. Merchant ships only made their way to the Northlands three or four times a year, so it could be spring or even summer before the message reached his brother-in-law. It mattered not. He still had one more campaign season, and he knew the letter would eventually reach Ana. She would know he was ready to leave the life of the legions behind. In his letter, Magnus asked Valens to implore Ana to join him in Britannia, and from there they would begin their life anew.

"Provided I survive," Magnus said, with a sudden feeling of foreboding. Over the years, he had seen the fates be both generous and cruel, in equal measure. Would Ana arrive in Britannia a year from now, only to find the father of her child had been slain in battle?

In Rome, the revelation that Scapula had claimed a sizeable gold mine in the mountainous reaches of western Britannia helped stem the growing criticism of his inability to bring the war against Caratacus to a decisive conclusion. Aulus Plautius, who led the imperial armies during the initial conquest and served as the first governor of Britannia, had been quick to defend his successor.

"The province is mostly volatile and untamed," he said, during a dinner party. The former commander-in-chief, who'd been lauded with *Triumphal Regalia* following the initial conquest, was hosting several honoured guests, including one of his former legates, Flavius

173

Vespasian. Also in attendance was the emperor's freedman, Narcissus, whom both Plautius and Vespasian viewed as a personal friend.

"I do not envy Scapula," the former legate remarked.

"The senate is filled with fat, pompous old fools who know nothing about conquering a new province," Plautius continued. "They give great speeches, but when the time comes for men to bleed, they are nowhere to be found."

"To be fair," Vespasian spoke up, "would you really want to trust the leading of our legions in battle to the majority of our senatorial colleagues?"

"Well stated," Narcissus remarked. He then decided to change the subject. "I hear, general, that the emperor has viewed you favourably regarding the consulship. It won't be for the coming year, unfortunately, but for the next year…"

"You flatter me," Vespasian replied, as he bit off a chunk of roasted chicken. "But I know the emperor. He awarded me *Triumphal Regalia* for our victories in Britannia, but he sees little use for me outside of being a soldier. If he is seriously considering nominating me for a future consulship, it is because his most trusted freedman has put the idea in his head. After all, I still believe it was you who convinced Claudius to give me command of the Second Legion during the invasion."

"An astute observation," Narcissus conceded, glancing away as Vespasian grinned at him knowingly. The former legate was a gruff soldier with a penchant for coarse language and crude humour. And he was far more intelligent and observant than he often let on. "Well," the freedman added, shrugging indifferently. "Consider it a birthday present."

"Yes, happy birthday, old man!" Plautius said, holding his wine chalice up in salute. "And how many is this for you?"

"Forty," Vespasian replied, feigning a glum demeanour. "I will be forty in three days."

"Well, time for you to start sporting some grey hairs, then!" Plautius, rapidly feeling the effects of wine, excused himself to go mingle with some of his other guests.

"Time for the truth, old friend," Vespasian said, once their host was out of earshot. "You influenced my promotion to legate, because you knew I could win battles. But why would you possibly

174

want me as one of the upcoming consuls? What's in it for Narcissus?"

"Safety in numbers, I suppose," the freedman confessed.

"Safety?" Vespasian asked, confused. "You are the emperor's most trusted advisor; the *'Right Hand of Caesar'*, as many say."

"I was, perhaps," Narcissus observed. He took another long pull off his wine.

Vespasian could see that he was clearly vexed.

"But I have always had friends within the inner circle. You don't think I brought down Messalina alone, do you?"

"I figured Pallas was involved."

"Of course he was! He wasn't one of Messalina's little fuck toys, so she couldn't control him. However, you may be surprised to know that Pallas and Agrippina are lovers."

"Hardly surprised," Vespasian scoffed. "He's been ploughing her hedge for years. Anyone with their eyes half-open could see that. But unlike Messalina, I don't think Claudius gives a damn who Agrippina spreads her legs for. With her being his niece and all, the thought of them shagging is rather revolting. This marriage has certainly been anything but popular among the masses. But what of it?"

"Agrippina is far more dangerous than you realize," Narcissus asserted. "Messalina was vindictive, but she was a fool and fairly easy to outwit. Claudius' blind love for her was the only weapon she had. Believe me when I say that Agrippina is twice as malicious as Messalina. She is also far more shrewd and intelligent, which makes her a lethal enemy."

"Yes, I did hear the emperor say he married her for her mind and not her heart," the former legate conceded.

"Her mind is what makes her frightening. I'll grant you, she advises our emperor well on most matters. And this gives her a far stronger hold on him than foolish love ever could."

"Personally, I find her insufferable," Vespasian remarked. "Mind you, she is attractive. Yet all I could ever see myself doing is shoving my cock in her mouth so she'll shut up."

This brought a much needed laugh from Narcissus.

"Anyway, what does all this have to do with you?"

"Everything and nothing. If Agrippina convinces the emperor my services are no longer needed, so be it. I am at his disposal and

175

would not object if compelled to take an early retirement. However, the rise of Agrippina has much to do with the emperor's son."

"Ah." Vespasian was suddenly understanding of the freedman's dilemma. He sat upright on his couch, hands folded in his lap. "Agrippina's son, Lucius, is the elder by three years. If Claudius adopts him, he will usurp Britannicus in the imperial succession."

"Treasonous harlot his mother may have been, but Britannicus is still the emperor's rightful son and heir," Narcissus stressed. He rolled onto his side and leaned in closer to his friend. "Did you know that insufferable brat, Lucius, has demanded he be allowed to change his name to Nero?"

"That doesn't surprise me," Vespasian grumbled. "Not only does the name mean 'strong', but by taking the name as the emperor's revered father, Drusus Nero, it would solidify his claim to the throne. It also strengthens the emperor's political alliances with Agrippina's supporters. But Lucius Domitius Ahenobarbus is no Nero. To allow him to take the name is a disgrace to all who earned it before him."

"It's not just the succession or what that brat chooses to call himself that worries me," Narcissus remarked. "It is the safety of the emperor's children. Claudius is not a young man and has never been in good health. Should he die before Britannicus comes of age, what will happen to him? And what of the emperor's daughters? I suspect Agrippina will try to convince him to marry her son to Octavia as soon as she's of legal age. Poor girl. I also suspect the empress views Lady Antonia as a political threat."

"Antonia is married to Faustus Sulla and not even living within the imperial household," Vespasian observed. "If anything, she is out of the way."

"She is very intelligent and extremely protective of her father. She proved a valuable source of information on the comings and goings of Messalina. I have little doubt that Agrippina knows this."

"You go too far now, old friend," Vespasian said, gently rebuking. "I understand your concerns for Britannicus and Octavia, but to think the empress will act against Antonia is downright paranoia."

"If you were in my position, would you not be a bit paranoid?"

"Probably," Vespasian conceded, before taking another drink of wine.

They could hear Plautius laughing boisterously down the hall and decided to quickly end their conversation.

"What would you have me do?"

"There is nothing you can do," Narcissus replied grimly. "For your own sake, stay clear of Empress Agrippina. You are one of Rome's greatest generals, but I know you struggle to keep your tongue in check."

"Don't worry, old friend," Vespasian said with a laugh, patting him on the shoulder. "I won't call Agrippina an insufferable twat unless seriously provoked!"

With the return of their host, thoughts turned to more sordid affairs. Plautius revealed he had acquired a bevy of dancers for their entertainment, as well as other pleasures should they feel especially indulgent. And while Flavius Vespasian was never one to turn down a healthy, vigorous shag, he found his mind was now miles away from Rome. There was little he could do for Narcissus except offer a friendly ear. The former legate's concerns now centred on a land he had done his best to help tame. He, like his former commander-in-chief, knew Britannia was anything but conquered.

Chapter XVII: Hard as Iron

Roman Camp at Viroconium, east of the River Sabrina
May 50 A.D.
***

Saturnalia, the winter solstice, and New Year came and went. The new consuls were a pair of rather unassuming senators named Antistius Vetus and Marcus Suillius. What intrigued Scapula and his legates, and indeed most of the army, was hearing that the emperor intended to share the consulship the following year with none other than the former legate of Legio II, Flavius Vespasian. But with the coming of spring, every Roman soldier in Britannia had more pressing matters than the intricacies of imperial politics.

There had been skirmishes on an almost daily basis since the frosts lifted. Their enemies only occasionally ventured across the Sabrina; however, they proved extremely aggressive, constantly ambushing any forays launched by Scapula's army. It was becoming apparent that Caratacus was hoping to draw the Romans into a decisive battle.

"Time to give him what he wants," General Paetus mused, during a meeting of senior officers.

A company of scouts had been dispatched, accompanied by Caratacus' brother, Amminus. A handful of supposed deserters told of the high king building a great stronghold at a place called Caer Caradoc. Amminus and the scouts return later that afternoon would confirm this. And while every other patrol across the river had been met with savage opposition, the hundred or so horsemen were left completely unmolested.

"Caratacus wants to be found," Paulinus surmised.

Amminus nodded in sombre confirmation.

"He may not have built a full-fledged fortress, but my brother was wise in his choice of ground," the Britannic prince reported. "There is only one way in. It's not too steep, but the ground is slippery with mud and smooth rocks. They've built a stone wall at the crest of a ridge."

A cavalry decurion added, "It's difficult to see because the forest is so damn thick, but it's definitely there."

"And there is no way around this?" Scapula asked.

Amminus shook his head slowly. "Not unless you want to send your forces ten miles up or down river. Even then, good luck navigating your way back to the battlefield. And the spurs of the hills are so heavily forested you won't be able to utilize your battle formations."

Paulinus stroked his chin for a moment. "If there is only one practicable way in, then it stands to reason there is only one way out."

"Yes," Amminus said, having come to the same conclusion as the legate. "Caratacus means to fight us here. There will be no retreat this time."

"All the same, we should get our light auxilia troops into the woods to surround the flanks of the stronghold," General Paetus pointed out. "They may intend to fight us, but once they break, we cannot allow the survivors to slip away."

Governor Scapula nodded. "Agreed. I am tired of chasing these people all over this damned isle."

"And I think my brother is tired of running from you," Amminus added. "Your tactics of burning villages and crops are forcing him to finally face us in battle. The Silures and Ordovices know their hit-and-run tactics are not sufficient. Doubtless many of their people starved this past winter, and Caratacus' fragile alliance will shatter if he does not give the people a major victory. I also heard rumour that his son, my dear nephew Jago, was killed during one of the ambushes last summer."

"A little personal vendetta will help compel him to fight," Scapula remarked with a dismissive shrug.

The corner of Amminus' mouth twitched at the governor's callousness, but he remained silent.

"How wide is the path leading up to the stronghold?" Paulinus asked the lead scout.

"About fifty feet, sir."

"That's pretty damn narrow," Paetus grumbled. "Even if the lead cohort attacks in close column, that's only enough spacing for fifteen soldiers in each rank."

"The ground on either side is thick with brush and undergrowth, but it is not impassable," the decurion spoke up. "It would be slower going, and formations would not be as tight, but it could be managed."

There were a few moments of silence. The senior officers contemplated their plan of attack.

Paulinus spoke up first. "Governor, I'll take the Twentieth up the middle. We'll attack in close order and undermine their defences. General Paetus and the Ninth Legion can assault on the wings."

Commander Julianus added, "Sir, I'll take my cavalry and several cohorts of auxilia infantry and move north to blockade any attempts at escape. The river veers westward a few miles from here, and there are a number of fording sites they could try to make use of."

Scapula nodded. "Have your men form a screen line along the hills overlooking the river. The Cornovii have promised to assist, but their warriors are neither well-trained nor particularly reliable. You have the rest of the day to get into position. The legions will attack at dawn."

It baffled Seisyll. Despite the terrible suffering their people endured through the previous winter, the Silures still preferred to fight a harassment war against Rome. His own Ordovices warriors were anxious to spill the blood of the invaders and had heeded his call in droves to come to Caer Caradoc. Only King Orin and five thousand men, mostly his personal guard, had come. This alone spoke volumes of the limited control he and Caratacus had over the fiercely independent Silures.

"My people's commitment has been four times that of Orin," Seisyll complained to the high king. "Even the Deceangli have sent nearly as many warriors as our friend, Orin."

"Orin himself stands with us," Caratacus said diplomatically. He was also flustered that only a fraction of the Silures fighters had come, but he knew nothing would be accomplished by squabbling between his two client kings.

"I don't doubt Orin's courage or his commitment to casting the Romans from our lands. But I do want your assurance that my people will be duly rewarded for the loyalty and courage they have shown."

"For their loyalty, and yours, you have my gratitude. As for your courage, you will have a chance to prove that soon, my friend."

Dawn came. With the quiet anticipation of the coming battle, the soldiers of the Twentieth Legion donned their armour, while centurions and their subordinate officers briefed the plans for the assault.

"Not very imaginative, is it?" Optio Caelius asked, with a trace of foreboding sarcasm.

"Caratacus has denied us any real chance of being creative here," Magnus reasoned. "Besides, there is a time and place for everything... even raw, brute force."

"And, of course, we in the First Cohort get the privilege of leading the assault."

"Would you rather we let some of the babies in the other cohorts, who've scarcely learned to shave, take the credit for breaking Caratacus? Or worse, lose the battle for us because they ran when it got rough?"

Caelius grinned appreciatively at his centurion's assessment. "I suppose it's time our men earn their incentive pay."

"Magnus!"

The Norseman turned to see Master Centurion Tyranus.

"You and Furius will take the lead. I will be immediately behind you. Once your centuries breach the defences, my lads will push through and create a break in their lines. The remaining centuries will be covering our flanks. Our intent is to rupture the walls and make enough space for the rest of the legion to form their battle lines."

"An ambitious plan," Magnus noted.

Tyranus smirked grimly. "Overly optimistic, probably, but it's what I put forth to General Paulinus. Most likely, this whole thing will turn into a bloody cluster-fuck before the day is done."

"Let's just hope it's Caratacus' men who do most of the bleeding," Magnus thought out loud.

The fleet-footed leader of Caratacus' scouts rushed to his high king and fell to one knee. "The Romans are coming, my king. One of their legions is clawing its way through the brush on either side of the road. The other is simply attacking straight at us."

"Harry them with missiles, but do not fall into a decisive engagement with them," Caratacus ordered. He turned to his horn blower. "Rally our warriors." The low, ominous blasts sounded and he took a deep breath. "And so the battle begins," he said softly.

"Form testudo!" Magnus and Furius ordered their centuries.

Shields were linked within the front rank, while those behind provided overhead protection. Being in such close quarters required even greater discipline, and keeping in step was crucial to maintaining formation integrity.

Arrows, throwing darts, and stones rained down upon the advancing legionaries. Just behind each century, trying to maintain a low profile as they advanced, were support companies of auxilia archers. Scapula had detached the majority in support of the Ninth Legion, who were spread out in a wide arc on either side of the path. The hundred or so who advanced in support of the Twentieth rose up, sending arrows flying back towards the scattered bands of warriors bombarding the legion. The dense foliage, uneven terrain, and scattered large boulders gave their adversaries ample cover to unleash repeatedly before being compelled to withdraw.

Hunkered behind his shield on the right edge of the front rank, Magnus could feel his hot breath deflecting off the inside of his shield. He had just enough of a gap to allow him to see. Despite the protection offered by his shield, the legionary behind, and his helmet, there was still the fear of an enemy arrow or dart finding its way into the narrow slit where his eyes were exposed. He spotted an Ordovices archer only thirty feet away who stepped out from behind a large rock and loosed his arrow at the centurion. Magnus ducked his head and grimaced as the arrow deflected off the brow of his helmet. He heard the legionary behind him yell, *'Fuck!'* in alarm. The centurion smiled as he saw his foe jolt backwards, an arrow from one of the auxilia archers protruding from his shoulder. There was a constant wave of arrows flying over their heads, the enemy missiles bouncing off or burying themselves in the cocoon of shields. Occasionally, Magnus would hear a yelp or cry, with no way of knowing if it was friendly archers or luckless legionaries being struck down.

The advancing soldiers kept their pace short and quick, careful not to slip on the slick rock or trip on protruding tree roots. Magnus took a deep breath as the wall came into sight. It appeared roughly eight feet tall and was made mostly of jagged flat rocks that permeated much of the landscape.

"First and second ranks, make ready to assault the wall. All other ranks...javelins ready!" The centurion then blew his whistle.

Under a fresh hail of stones and throwing spears, his men sprinted the rest of the way to the wall. Centurion Furius' century was following suit, the support archers close behind. Once there, the men in the second rank maintained their overhead cover, only now they braced their shields against the wall. Those in the front rank grounded their weapons and shields. They pulled on protruding stones, prying them loose with their pugio daggers, hoping to undermine the wall. The enemy warriors intensified their bombardment, smashing the covering shields with heavy rocks, buckling the legs of legionaries, and knocking others to their knees. Pila from their mates in the subsequent ranks were flung into the faces of their foes. Shrieks echoed as warriors were skewered by the fearful javelins. Spent pila also clattered against the wall, falling onto the protective shields of the second rank.

The exchange between the Ordovices and their Roman enemies was becoming more frenzied, warrior and soldier alike falling in the fearful exchange of arrow and spear. The rocks from barbarian slingers were the least imposing in appearance. Yet they inflicted some of the most fearful injuries, snapping limbs and breaking facial bones. And despite their armour and training, the Romans were at a disadvantage. Their enemies held the high ground, enjoying the protection offered by their makeshift wall. This made the task of Magnus and Furius' legionaries even more urgent.

The Norseman wrenched a loose stone free, tossing it aside. A few near eye level he managed to jerk from the wall. He saw the lower leg of an enemy skirmisher, standing atop an improvised timber platform. Magnus picked up his gladius and thrust it with all his might into the man's shin. The bone splintered as the sharpened point plunged deep into the limb. Magnus jerked the bloody weapon free, giving a malicious grin as the screaming warrior fell from the defences.

"They're pulling back, sir!" a decanus from the third rank shouted.

Magnus quickly glanced around, taking in his surroundings. The wall was beginning to crumble off to his left. To his right, the soldiers from Centurion Furius' century had collapsed part of the defences.

"Alright, lads!" the Norseman bellowed. "Let's knock the rest of this wall down!"

Their enemies having withdrawn, legionaries in the first two ranks braced their shields against the wall and shoved with all of their combined strength. With so much of the defences already dismantled, large breaches were created as sections of the wall collapsed inside the stronghold in a series of loud crashes.

"Century...on me!"

Caratacus' eyes were filled with hatred as he clutched his large broadsword in both hands. While Seisyll and the Ordovices fought to hold the ramparts on the wings, King Orin and his warriors stood near the high king, weapons banging on their shields as they worked themselves into a frenzy. Caratacus' gaze narrowed. He became fixated on the collapsing wall not thirty feet in front of him. Finally, his sword would sate its thirst for Roman blood. At last he would avenge his people, his brother...his son. A pang of sorrow stabbed at his heart as he thought about poor Jago. This was quickly channelled into the rage of vengeance.

"Aeron, guide my blade," he prayed through gritted teeth. *"Attack!"*

When his warriors charged, the Romans were still struggling over the crumbled remnants of the wall. This broke up their formations, preventing them from maintaining their shield wall. The force of the Silures' onslaught was blunted momentarily by the unleashing of the lead cohort's remaining javelins. Whether by luck or the hand of the gods, one such missile missed Caratacus' face by a matter of inches. The nearest warrior behind him was not so fortunate. The pilum plunged into his chest, snapping ribs and ripping into his left lung.

There would be time to mourn their fallen later. For now, Caratacus' heart was as cold as the steel blade he wielded. With a howl of rage echoing from the bowels of the underworld, he swung his weapon with every ounce of his power. It smashed into the shield of a legionary, the sharp blade cutting deep and knocking the man backwards. With alarming speed for a man of his size, the high king brought his sword around in a backhand swing, catching the soldier on the top of his helmet. The metal split and the legionary collapsed to the ground. Whether he was dead or simply rendered unconscious, Caratacus had no time to determine. One of the soldier's mates slammed the bottom edge of his shield into his stomach. The high king doubled over as he stumbled backwards, the wind knocked from him for a moment. He scowled in hatred, his fury coursing through his veins once more. He stormed forward with his blade held high, ready to stab, as one of his warriors attacked the soldier who'd smashed him with his shield. With the Romans scattered and struggling over the ruins, the legionary had no one on his left to protect him. This time there would be no doubt if his foe lived or died. Caratacus plunged his sword into the man's neck in a bursting spray of blood. The soldier collapsed in a convulsing heap as his life flowed onto the broken rocks. With animalistic lust, the high king ran his tongue over the bloodied blade, savouring the taste of his slain enemy.

Despite his triumph and brief taste of revenge, the imperial legionaries came onward. Their formations were coming together as they battled their way forward. Caratacus' warriors engaged them with bravery worthy of their ancestors. Many were paying the ultimate price for their valour. All knew the tribute demanded by the gods this day would be high, though the Roman gods would likely exact an equal toll from the legions. And while many of their brethren lay in bloody heaps, cries of agony through clenched teeth piercing the hills, those still standing stalwartly maintained their courage. The gods of war and death embraced this field of gore and visceral destruction.

The stubborn brawn and tenacity of the First Cohort had created the breach Scapula sought, though at a heavy price. As the follow-on cohorts stormed into the stronghold, they stumbled over scores of dead and badly injured legionaries. The auxilia archers had suffered greatly as well. Nearly half of their soldiers were struck down. The ground was slick with blood. In many cases, it was difficult to tell the wounded from the dying. Some were attempting to crawl away from the scene of death, covered in the mingling of blood from various friends and adversaries.

For Legate Suetonius Paulinus, the horrific carnage was the cost of his first true test as a legion commander. He dismounted his horse near the crumbled ruins of the wall and drew his spatha. Cohorts of legionaries were still clambering over the wreckage. Despite the protests of his staff officers, the commanding legate was determined to lead his men by example, rather than sitting on his horse well behind the actual fighting. To his right, he could see the cohorts from Legio IX battling their way into the stronghold. Those on the left were still struggling against the relentlessness of the barbarian defenders.

Paulinus grabbed the nearest pilus prior by the shoulder. It was Centurion Metellus of the Fifth Cohort. "I need you to take your cohort left, along the wall, and help the Ninth Legion."

"Yes, sir." Metellus stood on a pile of rocks and blew his whistle. "Fifth Cohort, action left! Battle formation on me!"

The battle was only now beginning for most of the legion. But for Centurion Magnus and the rest of the First Cohort, it had already been an exhausting and bloody day. As he blew his whistle, signalling the next *passage-of-lines*, he wondered if he'd lost more men this day than at Mai Dun or the Twin Rivers. Despite his personal tragedy, Mai Dun had been a brilliant piece of tactics and relentless valour. This battle, at a remote place called Caer Caradoc, had been little more than a bloody grind, degraded even further into an uncivilized brawl once the first blow was struck. Granted, there was little, if anything, about war that one could call 'civilized'.

Taking a moment to catch his breath, Magnus rapidly assessed his surroundings. Master Centurion Tyranus' century was on his immediate right, formed in a wedge that was pressing into the heart of the horde of enemy warriors. To his left, the cohort's Fifth Century was skirmishing with several bands of fighters.

Due to the rolling and extremely broken terrain, cohorts and even individual centuries were fighting their own battles, rather than the legion acting as a single entity. Just up ahead, about a hundred Ordovices warriors were attempting to make a stand atop a steep rock face, surrounded by an entire cohort of legionaries. Warrior and legionary were battling in a nearby ravine, while fighting continued on the upper reaches that lined the defilade. From the Norseman's position there was no way of telling who was winning. Most of the battles appeared to be at a stalemate. All he could do now was focus on his small piece of the overall struggle.

"Reform and advance!"

Caratacus stood atop a high outcropping of rock and surveyed the ongoing battle. The devolving of the clash into a series of separate engagements was just as unsettling for him as it was for the Romans. Because their numbers were so evenly matched, he did not have sufficient free warriors to swarm any of the imperial formations. King Orin and his Silures warriors were making the most determined stand in the very centre, hammering away at the large contingent of Roman soldiers. Only Caratacus' wife and daughter stood with him on the rock.

"A beautiful death," Eurgain said under her breath. Her face was painted with blue patterns. She carried a circular shield and a long spear. Her daughter's hand also clutched at the weapon. The queen was determined that should their people fall, all of their fates would be settled here. Such talk unnerved Caratacus, especially in light of his wife's refusal to find a safe shelter away from the fighting.

Satisfied there was little he could do except re-join the fray, the high king began to climb down the slope on the back side of the rock. As he reached the base, he was startled to see King Seisyll rushing towards him. His face was flushed and sweaty, his sword streaked with blood. The Ordovices king bore numerous injuries to his face, arms, and body. There was a nasty gash in his side that was seeping blood.

"Great king, I come to you for reinforcements!" Seisyll said urgently, his breath coming in gasps.

"Calm yourself, my friend," Caratacus replied, placing a hand on his shoulder to reassure him. "Tell me what has happened?"

"The Deceangli on our right flank have fled like cowards. Every last warrior I could muster is attempting to keep the Romans at bay, but they are crushing us both in front and on the right flank. We don't have the numbers to hold them!"

The news unnerved the high king. He supressed showing this outwardly. The Deceangli had brought four thousand warriors, and if they fled the balance of power had shifted decisively in the Romans' favour.

For Ostorius Scapula, he wasn't sure which was worse, not knowing how the battle was progressing or not being able to decide what actions he should take. The legions and auxilia cohorts had their orders. What else was he to do? He swallowed hard in trepidation as a rider from Paetus' legion rode quickly up the path towards him. His fears soon turned to relief and hope.

"Sir, compliments of General Paetus. He wishes to inform you that the enemy warriors on the extreme left have fled. Our soldiers are now pressing the enemy flank."

"Very good." The governor made an audible sigh. He signalled for his staff officers and escorts to follow him and kicked his horse into a canter.

He grimaced when he saw the first of the numerous bodies strewn along the road. "Send for the hospital wagons and surgeons," he ordered one of his messengers. Scapula cursed himself for not having done this sooner.

With Paulinus and Paetus commanding their legions, responsibility for tending to the wounded fell upon him. There were scores of maimed and injured men scattered about, most groaning or crying out piteously. Scapula knew casualties in the woods alongside the road were likely just as severe. He sent another rider back, to make certain the medics and stretcher bearers scoured the woods for fallen legionaries and archers.

As his horse stepped carefully over the ruins of the enemy defences, Scapula saw that despite the good news he'd received from Paetus, the battle was anything but decided. The crux of the struggle appeared to be taking place to his direct front, where the largest number of combatants on both sides were mustered. Five of the cohorts from Legio XX were formed into a massive front, battering away against a similar number of enemy warriors who, the governor was surprised to see, had yet to break. He was soon joined by General Paulinus. Strangely enough the legate was on foot, covered in sweat, grime and streaks of blood soiling his otherwise ornate armour.

"Governor, glad to have you with us."

"Paetus has turned the left flank," Scapula informed him. "How are your men holding up?"

"They're pretty fucking spent, sir," Paulinus replied bluntly. "But they have enough left in them to break this lot. Can't say we'll have much left in us for a pursuit."

"Winning the battle will be enough," the governor reassured him. They looked to see that the walls of warriors and legionaries were still punishing each other, even as centurions tried to keep rotating fresh lines of troops into the fray. The governor then added with begrudging respect, "These bastards are as hard as iron."

Chapter XVIII: A Triumph of Steel

***

Ostorius Scapula was willing to give his adversaries a certain measure of respect for their valour and tenacity, yet Caratacus felt only hatred and frustration towards his foe. Even if the Deceangli had not fled like cowards, the Roman tactics allowed them an advantage when it came to close-combat fighting. His warriors expended huge amounts of energy trying to break the legions' shield walls. The imperial soldiers were far more measured and deliberate, though they certainly did not lack in ferocity. What gave them the advantage, besides the superior protection offered by their shields and armour, was the constant rotation of their battle lines. It was mind-numbingly frustrating for his warriors to watch. Every few minutes, the enemy centurions gave the order. Their battered soldiers would withdraw to the rear of their formations and rested legionaries would smash their way into the ongoing brawl.

With so many factors now working against his warriors, Caratacus saw that casualties were starting to mount as his exhausted fighters fell in the onslaught of legionary blades. Enemy archers were also scattered about in small bands, unleashing their arrows on exposed warriors occupying the patches of high ground. The high king understood there could be no retreat, not now. The Silures in particular would condemn him for cowardice. The bravest of all his warriors, he quietly cursed that there were not more of them on this battlefield.

"Sire, King Orin has fallen!"

The voice of a near panicked warrior alerted Caratacus, and he rushed over to where a dozen men carried their king away from the fighting. He had been impaled through the bowels by a legionary gladius, leaving him in hellish agony. He gritted his teeth, refusing to cry out despite the unholy pain.

"Orin," Caratacus said, kneeling and taking him by the hand.

Blood and bile erupted from the Silures king's mouth. "I am sorry," he whispered. "Sorry that I will not be h…here to witness your victory over the Romans."

Caratacus patted him on the shoulder and ordered the small band of warriors, "Get him to safety, as far from here as possible."

"Yes, sire."

"We will not let the Romans take him."

Caratacus took a deep breath, channelling his rage once more. There was only one thing left for him to do... fight!

Magnus slammed his shield boss into the face of an exhausted enemy warrior before stabbing the man in the guts. As spent as he and his men were, fatigue was an even more critical factor for their enemies. The Silures were some of the bravest adversaries he had ever faced, yet even they were being compelled to give ground against the legion's relentless assault. Bodies of the fallen were becoming a hazardous and ever-growing obstacle, as legionary and warrior fell in the frenzy of blood and steel. The legion continued its methodical advance. Soldiers in the subsequent ranks stabbed the enemy fallen, ensuring they were dead.

"Onward, lads!" Magnus shouted, as much for his own benefit as his soldiers'. "They're breaking!"

Governor Scapula rode down the vast battle front. He saw, in addition to Paetus' men folding in the extreme flank of their enemy, individual cohort battles were slowly being decided. Warriors on the numerous knolls and outcroppings were wearing down under the constant attack of legionaries, while being harried by volleys of arrows. Small bands of Ordovices warriors began to break and run, then larger groups. Scapula kicked his horse into a gallop, to see what was happening on the right of the battle line. It seemed the entire enemy force was now in full flight. There had been no one decisive moment when their will shattered; the Romans had simply ground them into submission through brute force. Only the valiant Silures continued to battle, but even they could not hold for much longer.

"General Paulinus!" Scapula shouted to the legate who appeared to be engaging the enemy alongside his First Cohort.

"Sir?" Paulinus asked, sprinting back to the governor. Despite his exhaustion, he was grinning from ear-to-ear. The thrill of battle had, for the moment, overwhelmed any sense of revulsion at the terrible carnage.

"The Ordovices are on the run; the Ninth Legion is driving them from the field. Send all cohorts that are not directly engaged to hit the Silures on the flanks."

Paulinus waved for his servant to bring his horse. He quickly surveyed the scene before sending two of his staff tribunes with orders to the outermost cohorts.

Centurion Metellus Artorius and the Fifth Cohort found themselves on the extreme left of the legion, following their clearing of the ramparts in support of the Ninth Legion. The small hills and rock outcroppings made it impossible for him to see what was transpiring off to the right. For him and his legionaries, the battle was still a chaotic mess, albeit one with far fewer enemies to face them now.

"Centurion Metellus!" the staff tribune called to him.

Too tired to salute, Metellus nodded in acknowledgment.

"Orders from General Paulinus. You're to take your men and swing around the flank of the centre Silures force. They are all that remains on the field."

"Excellent," the centurion replied, with a tired smile. "My compliments to the legate. Tell him we're on our way and will hit these bastards from the flank and behind." He turned to face his men. *"Fifth Cohort, reform battle lines! On my command...at the double-time...march!"*

Caratacus continued to swing his sword against the Roman shield wall, yet his blows lacked the speed or intensity of his earlier strikes. He had succeeded in felling a legionary with a blow to the crown of his helmet, but he and his surviving warriors were fast succumbing to the wall of steel. His fighters were falling at a rapid rate, fatigue muffling their screams through the constant stabbing of legionary blades. The high king stumbled backwards up the gentle slope and gazed over his shoulder, his eyes widening in horror. With their flank support gone, his wife and daughter were now under assault from a swarm of legionaries. Eurgain wielded her spear with bravery and skill. Yet, it was only a matter of moments before the bottom edge of a shield was slammed into her forehead, splitting her scalp and dropping her to her knees. Young Sorcha had been kicked hard in the stomach by one of those vile creatures. Caratacus' greatest fears were unfolding before his eyes.

"No!" he screamed.

At that moment, what little resolve remained among the Silures shattered.

An organized pursuit was proving impossible. Paulinus suspected as much, for the legions were too exhausted to commit to chasing down the hordes of fleeing enemy warriors. And while the light auxilia were scattered about the woods and hills, they were too few in number to capture or kill more than a handful of enemies. What mattered now to Scapula and his legates was finding Caratacus.

"Stop!" Amminus shouted.

He rushed over to the legionary who smashed Eurgain with his shield. The soldier had his gladius raised high, ready to plunge the blade into the woman's neck.

"What the fuck do you care?" the soldier spat.

"This is Caratacus' wife. She is worth more to us alive than dead." Amminus knelt and raised the chin of sister-in-law he had not seen in many years. He reckoned the terrified little girl clutching Eurgain's hand was his niece, whom he had never even met. "Hello, sister," he said in their native tongue.

Eurgain spat onto the ground. Her left eye was closed, her face and forehead covered in blood. "Our traitorous kinsman has returned to us."

"Come, dear sister." Amminus stood and offered her his hand. "Let us fight no more."

Eurgain looked around her and saw nothing but growing numbers of Roman soldiers. Were it not for her daughter, she would have attacked her brother-in-law with her bare hands and made the Romans kill her. She did not know if her husband was dead, captured, or fled. All she knew in that moment was Sorcha needed

193

her mother. She reluctantly accepted Amminus' outstretched hand, allowing him to pull her to her feet. She swooned for a moment, the effects of her injury nearly overwhelming her.

"Come, I've got you," Amminus said, placing an arm around her shoulder.

"Don't think this lessons the hate I feel for you."

"Who is he, Mother?" Sorcha asked, clutching her frock and staring nervously at the strange man, eyes wide.

Before Eurgain could answer, Amminus said, "I am your uncle, dear child. And I have come to take you away from this place of misery and pain."

They were escorted across the expanse of broken bodies and gory aftermath of battle to where Scapula, his legates, and their senior officers were gathering.

"Noble Governor," Amminus announced. "I have brought you Caratacus' wife and daughter. I ask that you see to my sister-in-law's injuries and take care of them. Though her husband may be our enemy, these two are still my kin."

"Of course," Scapula said. He pointed to one of the staff officers. "Have the medics see to her injuries then escort them to my tent. Amminus, tell them they will be my guests, and will be treated with respect."

Amminus translated the message. Eurgain's loathing for the Romans was in no way dissipated, but she took some solace in knowing her daughter would be safe.

Despite his injuries and roving patrols of Roman auxiliaries, King Seisyll had little difficulty navigating through the woods to safety. The imperial cavalry was concentrated mostly northeast of the River Sabrina. Yet to the northwest it was relatively quiet. A small footbridge spanned the river, concealed by a thick grove of trees. It appeared to be unknown to the Romans. On the other side, he found the remnants of a band of Silures. They were gathered protectively around a makeshift litter, upon which lay the mortally wounded King Orin. The battered warriors bowed their heads in respect as Seisyll walked through their circle and knelt next to his fellow king.

"My friend," he said, placing a hand on Orin's arm.

His skin was cold and clammy. Given the severity of his hideous wound, it was no small wonder he was still alive.

"Seisyll." His voice was scarcely more than a whisper. "The battle…was it…"

The Ordovices king was tempted to reassure Orin that the battle had been won, but knew better than to treat him with such disrespect. "I am sorry," he replied. "Even Caratacus could not withstand the Romans."

"I thought not." Orin swallowed hard. It pained him to do so. His lips were covered in spittle and dried bile which had run down his chin. "I fear what will happen to our peoples." His strength failing, he extended his hand upwards.

Seisyll clasped it firmly.

"I go now to stand before the gods. I hope they will find favour in the manner of my death. I ask your pardon for any wrongs I have committed in this life, so we may depart as friends."

"Of course." Seisyll fought back tears. His sorrow for their fallen comrades now beginning to overwhelm him. Orin had been his rival and one time enemy. Through Caratacus he had come to view the Silures king as a noble and worthy friend. His dignity and the manner of his pending death endeared him to the Ordovices king.

"Promise me one thing," Orin whispered. He fought to delay his passing for just a moment longer. "Promise you will never stop fighting, not until Silures and Ordovices are free."

"I promise." Seisyll hoping to reassure his fellow king.

Orin gave a short cough, his final breath sputtering past his lips, and his hand fell limp from Seisyll's grasp.

"Rest well, brave son of Silures." With a last show of respect, he kissed the slain king upon the forehead and then stood. Though determined to keep his promise, he was at a complete loss as to what to do.

Caratacus was missing. If he were slain or captured, the alliance between Silures and Ordovices would crumble. Seisyll feared it may be doomed anyway. His surviving warriors would blame their southern neighbours for this defeat. He felt the same as he gazed upon the sullen faces of Orin's defeated bodyguards. Had the Silures war chiefs not been so reluctant to face the Romans in open battle, had they committed as strongly as his own Ordovices, they could have overwhelmed the invaders by sheer force of numbers. The Battle of Caer Caradoc had not been determined by skill or bravery, but by which force was able to grind the other down first. With an additional ten thousand Silures warriors, it would have been the Romans who broke this day!

Seisyll took a deep breath and shook his head. He knew it was pointless to speculate on what might have been. He had to face reality. The Silures had not stood with them against the Romans. Their king was now dead, and the high king likely captured or killed. Seisyll then decided he would return to his great hall, rally his people in defence of their own lands, and by their strength alone would continue to battle against the invaders.

For Magnus it was a strange feeling, the aftermath of this battle. There was the contrasting amalgamation of triumph and sorrow; and yet there was something else he could not quite explain. A sense of closure came over him, like his very soul knew this was his final battle. He closed his eyes. A gentle breeze blew over his face. As he raised his head towards the heavens, he swore he could hear a woman's voice on the wind.

Well done, my love. Now be at peace, Soldier of Rome.

Chapter XIX: Freedom or Slavery

Kingdom of the Brigantes
30 May 50 A.D.
***

For Caratacus, the days following the battle were a blur filled with sorrow, anger, hunger, and exhaustion. It was eighty miles to his destination, and he was devoid of a horse. He knew time was against him. He had to reach Venutius as soon as possible. He kept to the woods, following the narrow and rarely used paths of huntsmen, only sleeping when he collapsed and could go no further. The only food he ate consisted of berries and unripe fruit. On the second night of his trek, he managed to snare a hare. With a lack of implements to make fire he was forced to consume his meal raw. It did little to ease his hunger pangs, and instead made him ill. He pressed on, intent on reaching the Kingdom of Brigantes. He loathed the thought of asking that bitch, Cartimandua, for aid. But, it was the only hope he had for Eurgain and Sorcha. In his tired and desperate mind, he hoped Venutius had finally compelled his wife to come to her senses regarding the Roman scourge.

Far from compelling his wife, the queen, to stand against the Romans, the relations between Cartimandua and her consort had become even more strained. They rarely spoke anymore. However, there would be plenty of words exchanged the day Caratacus boldly came into their great hall at the royal court. They had been discussing a land dispute with a pair of farmers. All was immediately forgotten as the doors were flung open.

"It cannot be," the queen said with quiet apprehension.

Venutius smiled, glad to see his friend especially after receiving news of his terrible defeat.

Caratacus had taken the time to wash the blood and filth from his face and body, yet there was no mistaking his tired and haggard appearance. He walked confidently, his head held high, to the queen and her consort.

Venutius rose from his seat and bowed. "We welcome you, Caratacus, High King of Catuvellauni, Silures, and Ordovices."

"Sit down, husband," Cartimandua ordered him, her voice cool with a trace of bitterness. She gazed at their unexpected guest. "Caratacus is *not* King of Catuvellauni, though I will not dispute his titles from across the Sabrina. However, I do know he is both murderer and inciter of war. So tell me, Caratacus, son of Cunobeline, why do you enter my hall?"

"To plead for your help, my lady," Caratacus bowed humbly. While he found it degrading, he knew Cartimandua was his only chance at salvation.

"And we should give it to you," Venutius spoke up quickly.

He drew an icy glare from his wife, meeting her gaze with a scornful scowl of his own.

"Caratacus shares the blood of all our ancestors. The Romans have left desolation in the lands west of the Sabrina. We *must* offer him our aid and protection."

"The west of the Sabrina belongs to the Silures and Ordovices," Cartimandua reminded him. "These people have burned our farms and murdered our people. Caratacus has sought to compel us through terror. While I admire his determination and courage, I think there is someone he should speak with first." She signalled to one of her guardsmen. He beat the butt of his spear against the ground three times. Venutius and Caratacus were horrified to see Amminus enter the hall, accompanied by a dozen Roman cavalry soldiers.

"Brother," he said, his face tight with strain.

"What is the meaning of this?" Venutius demanded. "Why is *he* here?"

"Why, indeed." Caratacus closed his eyes in resignation. When he opened them again, they were filled with rage. *"Wicked bitch!"*

Before he could draw his blade, troopers surrounded him. It took two men to hold each arm, and another to seize his weapon.

"What are you doing?" Venutius stood, his face red with anger. "You don't mean to let the Romans have him?"

Cartimandua glanced at him for a moment before turning to her guard's captain. "Take him away and chain him…and have my husband escorted from the hall. He is not well and needs his rest."

Venutius spat at her feet. A guard placed a hand on his shoulder, only to have the consort smack it away. His expression turned to one of sadness as he and Caratacus locked eyes for a brief moment.

"I am sorry, my friend."

As Caratacus was led away, shouting curses at his brother and Cartimandua, Amminus could clearly see the signs of strain on the queen's face. Still a very striking woman, lines had begun to form prematurely around her eyes and across her brow. Her face seemed in pain from constant the tightness in her jaw.

"You realize what a predicament this puts me in," she said. "We may be in an alliance with Rome, but many of my people revere Caratacus as a hero and fighter for liberty. And as you saw, my husband considers your brother to be a very close friend."

"Too close," Amminus reasoned.

"And that is why you have put me in a very precarious position. By Freya, you knew Caratacus was coming this way! Why did you not intercept him with cavalry?"

"I sympathize with you. However, we had to be certain to capturing him and not let him slip away. Had he seen a regiment of imperial horsemen waiting for him, he would have disappeared. Like he's done numerous times already. Whatever your internal political difficulties, giving the Romans their most sought-after prize will make you the most powerful client monarch in all Britannia. Emperor Claudius is both wise and generous; that you give him Caratacus rather than being coerced by his serpent's tongue will be met with much generosity."

The queen reluctantly understood. Despite the promises of wealth and aid from the Romans, it would amount to little if she were usurped by her own disaffected nobles. Amminus recognized this and could not help but goad Cartimandua further.

"Learn to control your people, especially that barbarian you call 'husband'. You have the chance to become Caesar's strongest ally in these lands. It would be a shame to lose it all."

Cartimandua's gaze narrowed, her voice like ice. "Do not threaten me, Amminus. You are foolish, indeed, if you think the Romans would ever place you upon the throne of any kingdom within Britannia, least of all mine. I have made good on my promises to the emperor, and you have your prize. Leave now, and do not return."

"Apologies, my lady," Amminus said, with a short, patronizing bow. "I meant no offence. I know I don't need to tell you that your safety, and that of your kingdom, depend on you keeping your consort and his barbaric dogs in check."

"I understand far more than you realize." The queen's voice had softened. She was willing to give Amminus the benefit of the doubt. Surely he could not be so foolish as to infer that the Romans would ever consider him a viable ruler of the Brigantes. No, the real threat to her kingdom came not from Rome nor from a disgraced former Catuvellauni prince. And though she loathed to admit it, Amminus was right; the imperial governors would only go so far to keep her secure upon the Brigantes throne. She knew she needed to deal with Venutius sooner rather than later.

Three days later, a courier delivered the news to Governor Scapula. Caratacus had been captured, and a contingent of cavalry from Legio XIV was accompanying him to Camulodunum. Word spread quickly, soldiers breaking into celebration at the news. The war had ended for the time being. But, there was much to be done if western Britannia was to be fully absorbed into the Roman province.

"I want arrangements made for our guests' transfer to Rome as soon as possible," Scapula said to Admiral Stoppello. "The emperor's birthday falls on the Calends of August, and I think Caratacus will make a fine prize and birthday present for him."

"I'll take him to Rome, personally," the admiral replied. "Provided the weather cooperates, we should reach Ostia in two, maybe three weeks' time."

"He'll have just enough time to get over being seasick before being strangled for the amusement of the mob," Paulinus added with morbid humour.

"Feeling merciful, general?" one of Scapula's aids asked.

Paulinus shook his head. "No, just making an observation is all. Caratacus was a worthy adversary, but so was Vercingetorix. And we all know what happened to him."

"The Divine Julius was merciful enough to have him strangled in prison rather than before the people," Scapula remarked. Though very much relieved to hear of Caratacus' capture, the governor was feeling the strains of office in this ever-volatile province. He hoped to continue the subjugation of the western reaches during the next campaign season, though he knew that capturing Caratacus would not end the struggles with the Silures and Ordovices. He was further concerned by rumours of unrest among the Iceni and other tribes in the east. Despite the troubles he had taken in capturing Caratacus, in that moment Scapula did not want to deal with him. He would send their prize captive to Rome for the amusement of the mob, to be disposed of as the emperor saw fit.

Chapter XX: Heart of the Empire

Rome
20 July 50 A.D.
***

The voyage by sea had been long and insufferable for Caratacus and his family. They were confined to their cabin for the most part, only allowed on the aft deck when they needed to relieve themselves. Though not kept in chains, a pair of armed marines remained outside the bolted door to their cabin at all times. The only joy the newly deposed high king felt was in being reunited with his wife and daughter once more. At least a score of various captured nobles had been sent to Rome with them. They were kept below deck in a makeshift brig.

The ship would stop in various ports along the way, and Caratacus would stare out the small window, wishing he could break down the door and escape with his family. He had no idea where they were, but he did not care. All that mattered now was keeping Eurgain and Sorcha safe. Yet, how safe could any of them be when they were prisoners of Rome? With great despair, they arrived in the port of Ostia nearly two months after his capture. As they were led out onto the deck, with nearly a hundred armed soldiers waiting for them, Caratacus caught his first glimpse of the distant imperial capital. He closed his eyes and breathed in the warm, humid sea air. He then accepted whatever the gods decreed for him. Whatever fate awaited him and his family, he would face it like a man and a king.

Empress Agrippina was thrilled to hear that the barbarian king had come to Rome. She pleaded with her husband to be allowed to have a private audience with Caratacus prior to his addressing of the emperor and senate. While Claudius found this to be rather absurd, he knew it was not worth the pending argument if he were to refuse her. Besides, there was no harm in allowing his wife the pleasure of having a captive ruler prostrate himself before her. Caratacus was a dead man, after all. Like Vercingetorix before him, he would be paraded through the streets of Rome in chains, after which he would be strangled for the amusement of the mob. His wife and daughter would likely suffer a similar fate, unless some wealthy senator offered up enough coin to purchase them as his personal slaves. While it was possible someone with enough denarii would fancy having the daughter of a defeated king within his household, taking the fallen queen as a slave would likely prove more trouble than the novelty was worth.

The empress found her husband in his study where he spent most of his evenings. Claudius had proven to be quite the scholar, even in his youth when most dismissed him as a half-wit. Rumour had it he was currently writing a history of the Julio-Claudians, as well as his autobiography. However, he kept a close hold on his current works and allowed no one to see his writings, not even his wife or most trusted advisors. As Agrippina let herself into the study, Claudius hurriedly covered up the scroll he'd been working on.

"Hard at work, dear husband?" she asked in a sultry voice. The emperor may have married her for her mind, but he was still a man, and just as prone to the machinations of an attractive woman.

"Y…yes," he stammered. "What is it you w…want?"

"Oh, can I not come visit my dear, dear husband, who I almost never see?" Agrippina sat on his lap and ran her fingers through his hair.

Strangely enough, the fact that he was her uncle had never bothered her nor had the public revulsion at their union. She was the type who rarely had sex strictly for pleasure. Certainly, she enjoyed it in a purely physical sense, but she was no nymphomaniac like Messalina. For Agrippina, the real pleasure came from using her more exotic talents as the ultimate weapon of control, and she would use them on anyone, man or woman, it mattered not.

Claudius appreciated her skills at love-making. He also knew that she rarely came on to him unless she wanted something in return. "Oh come now, y…you are only so giving of yourself when you w…want something."

"Dear husband, you know me too well." The empress laughed, its tone was both playful and condescending, in equal measure. She continued to stroke his hair as she cut to the chase. "That barbarian king is to be granted an audience with the senate tomorrow."

"Yes. Caratacus asked to address the senate, and I have granted this out of respect for a w…worthy adversary."

"I want him first," Agrippina said coldly. She slapped Claudius gently on the chest when he raised an eyebrow. "Not in *that* fashion, you silly fool!" She was then serious, her demeanour cold and determined. "I am Empress of Rome and the senate loathe and disrespect me. Let me have my audience with Caratacus first, in the foyer of the senate, before he comes before them. Give me this, and let those back-biting cowards see your fallen enemies prostrate themselves before me. I cannot serve you best as consort if I am not given proper deference and respect by the senate."

While Claudius disdained the thought of inflating his wife's already profound ego, he knew she was right. If she was to best serve as consort of the empire, the senate would have to be humbled ever so slightly, that they may give proper respect to their empress. Having Caratacus offer supplication to Agrippina would make his point clear without causing disrespect among the senate.

"Very well, my dear," Claudius said, placing both arms around her waist. "B…before Caratacus offers his submission to emperor and senate, he shall first offer his respects to the Empress of Rome." He stood and began to usher her into his bedroom down the hall. Claudius was not feeling particularly amorous this evening; however, he had just written some rather abrupt descriptions of both his wife and her son in his memoir, which he did not wish for her to see, for none of it was remotely flattering to either.

There was an air about Caratacus of both defiance as well as acceptance for whatever fate the gods dealt him. In his heart, he knew he had fought well against the Romans, and surely his gods would reward his courage and loyalty to their people. On this day, he was dressed in a newer tunic with his tartan cloak over his left shoulder. He bathed that morning, with his hair and thick moustache covered in a greyish dye. His hair was spiked, like some sort of crown. Eurgain and Sorcha were both bathed and well-dressed in Roman style stolas. The queen detested being clothed in a manner similar to their enemies.

"Why are we doing this?" Eurgain asked, as they waited to be escorted into the senate. "Let the Romans kill us and be done with it."

"No, my love," Caratacus replied. "I want to look their emperor in the eye and let him know what sort of enemy he has faced these past seven years. I want him to lie awake at night, fearful his suppression of our people will lead to death of his beloved empire. Rome is a vast city of beauty I have not been able to comprehend, yet it is ruled by monsters. They can kill me if they wish, but I will not go quietly to my execution."

Eyes wet with tears, her face beaming with pride, Eurgain placed her hands on either side of her husband's face and kissed him deeply. Though she longed to follow their son into the afterlife, they would do so on their terms and not the Romans'.

They were escorted by a dozen heavily armed soldiers. They came into a foyer where a woman in resplendent robes sat atop a dais, a golden laurel crown atop her head.

"The empress," Eurgain whispered.

Agrippina said nothing. She stared in amusement at the gathering of barbarian nobility.

Caratacus was fluent in the Roman tongue, and he stepped forward and gave a respectful bow to the empress consort. "My lady," he said. "Your beauty enhances that of your eternal city."

"Your repute for bravery and nobility precedes you," Agrippina replied. "I am glad to see your reputation is well-founded."

Caratacus bowed once more before he and his entourage were escorted into the senate chamber proper. Every bench in the house was crammed with senators anxious to cast their eyes on the man who caused them such grief in Britannia. Their faces bore expressions that varied from curious to scowls of disgust. The guards halted the procession at the entrance for a brief moment so the porter could announce them.

At the end of the hall sat Emperor Claudius and the two consuls. It was the first time Caratacus had seen the Emperor of Rome, and he was puzzled by what he saw. Claudius appeared to be a frail old man, scarcely the divinity the Romans professed. Like the empress, he wore a crown upon his head, made of actual laurel leaves rather than gold. His gold-lined purple robes were magnificent, and Caratacus could only guess their value. He jolted as the porter beat his staff on the ground three times in a loud echo across the marble floor.

"Caratacus, son of Cunobeline, Prince of the Catuvellauni, and High King of the Silures and Ordovices!"

A praetorian shoved him forward. The chamber was silent as a tomb as the high king, his family, and a handful of nobles made their way towards the raised steps where the emperor sat.

"Kneel," a guardsman said sternly, pointing to the floor.

Caratacus nodded to his entourage, who reluctantly knelt with their heads bowed. Eurgain closed her eyes, disgusted at being humbled this way but she complied. Only Caratacus remained standing.

"Caesar," Caratacus began, speaking slowly and attempting to stifle his accent, while adding force to his words. "I stand before you as a humbled and defeated, yet worthy, enemy. You address me as a high king, yet if the degree of my nobility had been matched by moderation in success, I would have come to this city as a friend rather than a captive enemy. Nor would you have disdained to receive in peace one whose noble ancestors lorded over a great many nations. Therefore my present lot, humbling as it is for me, is so much more the magnificent triumph for you. I had horses, men, arms, and wealth. Does it really surprise you that I should be unwilling to lose these? You wish to rule over the world, yet what surprise that many will not accept your slavery? You take lands with the sword and by doing so I urge you to heed this warning. Be prepared to sleep with your sword, ever a watchful eye gazing into the night, for you shall need it!"

Caratacus expected to be rebuked by this time, but there were no immediate responses from the emperor or assembled senators. Indeed, Flavius Vespasian and Aulus Plautius appeared to be grinning in appreciation. The host of senators seemed shocked by his stern and defiant tone, for they had expected him to prostrate himself before the emperor and beg for mercy.

Caratacus softened his tone and continued, "If I were now being handed over as one who had immediately capitulated, or had I supplicated myself before you following the death of my noble brother, neither my fortune nor your glory would have achieved any brilliance at all. How noble is an enemy who refuses to fight for the freedom of his people? By standing against Rome, I am damned.

206

Reprisal will be followed by oblivion." He paused for effect, glancing around the room before fixing his gaze on the emperor. "On the other hand, if you preserve me, mortal enemy that I have been, I shall be an eternal example of your clemency. Perhaps, then, Rome will have demonstrated that she is a rightful and just ruler of the world."

He folded his arms, a sign that he was finished, his eyes still fixed on Claudius who appeared to have had no reaction at all to the speech. Had he fumbled the Latin words? Did it all come across as gibberish, or did the Romans simply not care at all about nobility and sacrifice? Were they truly the vile dogs he described them as?

It was Vespasian and Plautius who answered those questions. They stood and started to slowly clap their hands together. The emperor at last smiled and gave a nod of approval before adding his own clapping to the growing applause. The terrified barbarian nobles at Caratacus' feet, who'd been unable to understand a word of his speech, dared to look up in wonder. The entire Senate of Rome was on its feet, loudly and boisterously applauding the speech of the most dangerous enemy in recent memory. Claudius finally stood and raised a hand, silencing the host of senators.

"Noble Caratacus," he said, speaking slowly so as to stifle his natural stammer. "You come before us with dignity and grace worthy of your noble ancestors, and that of a true Britannic king. The power of Rome lies not with the sword but with civility and justice. Your words have moved me, as they have every member of this august assembly. And through our clemency will the greatness of both our people's be realized."

The emperor slowly descended the steps. Caratacus towered over him and looked as if he could snap him like a twig. However, it was Claudius, not he who wielded power in Rome. The emperor gazed up at him for a moment before smiling to the prostrate Britannic nobles and waving for them to rise. All did so, their expressions showing a profound sense of bemusement.

"We are free to go?" Caratacus asked hesitantly.

"Sadly, we cannot allow you to return to Britannia," Claudius answered. "But that does not mean you are slaves or prisoners. You will be my guests with a villa in Rome to call your new home."

For Centurion Primus Ordo Magnus Flavianus, his departure from the legions was a very quiet and private affair. Rather than having an elaborate ceremony, as was the norm for senior-ranking centurions, Magnus had simply taken his discharge and retirement orders from the legion's aquilifer and shared a few words with General Paulinus. The evening prior he said his farewells to the men of his century. He left before dawn, having instructed Optio Caelius to assume command of the century until his replacement was appointed.

By chance, he had received a reply back from Tiberius Valens just prior to his departure. Ana and young Titus had taken a ship that landed not at Camulodunum but at Aqua Sulis, where they were the guests of the mayoral magistrate, Aulus Cursor. The now former centurion primus ordo saddled his horse and made the journey from the legion's camp to the home of Britannia's legendary hot springs. It took him three days to make the trek, and for Magnus it felt like three lifetimes.

He had only been to Aqua Sulis once before, soon after the initial invasion. While still very primitive, there were definite signs of 'Romanization'. The River Abona brought much in the way of merchant traffic from the continent, and the docks were teaming with activity. Most of the roads were still dirt paths, but at least they were kept free of weeds and debris. Fosse Way, which connected the southwestern coast with many of the Roman towns leading into Catuvellauni and Brigantes, was the only paved road in the region.

A military fort had been erected near the northeast corner of the springs which were a series of pools locals used for bathing. The fort housed two cohorts of auxilia infantry as well as a small detachment of cavalry. Near the fort was the mayor's residence; a magnificent villa that stood in stark contrast to the more austere buildings of the town. Aulus Cursor was rather ambitious when it came to his plans for Romanizing Aqua Sulis. Magnus noted, such assimilation of architecture and culture would take years, possibly decades.

He dismounted near the gates of the villa where a pair of auxilia troopers were on duty. It was the first time in many years soldiers had not come to attention and saluted him.

"Can we help you?" one of the men asked.

Though the Norseman now wore a plain, brown tunic, he still kept his gladius strapped to his hip, and the troopers were both staring at its rather ornate scabbard.

"Magnus Flavianus, recently retired centurion primus ordo of the Twentieth Legion and friend of Aulus Cursor. My wife and son are his guests." It felt strange calling Ana as his wife. He wasn't sure how else to refer to her.

"Beg your pardon, sir," the first trooper said, coming to attention. "You may enter."

Magnus almost saluted, then stopped himself and grinned.

"Old habits die hard, sir," the soldier said with an appreciative smile.

The grounds of the mayor's villa were still a work-in-progress, though they did have a very splendid garden, complete with well-groomed hedges and various shrubberies. He heard the excited cries of a child, and his face was beaming as he saw the little boy, not even a year old yet already able to walk, running through the gardens, laughing all the while.

"Where are you?" His mother's voice called playfully from the other end of a hedge.

The boy hid behind a stone bench, then turned and ran straight into Magnus' arms. He gave a startled shriek at first, but then giggled as he apprised the big Norseman who held him. His expression was one of curiosity and devoid of fear.

"By Odin and Jupiter," Magnus said quietly. He heard a startled yelp as Ana came around the corner.

Her hands were over her mouth, eyes wide.

"Hello, Ana. I seem to have met young Titus."

Without a word, she rushed forward and wrapped her arms around them both, kissing Magnus on the lips and face.

"I wasn't sure if I'd ever see you again," she said breathlessly. "I heard there was a terrible battle, and that Caratacus was defeated, but no one could tell me if you were alive or dead."

"Very much alive," Magnus reassured her with a chuckle. "And no longer a soldier of Rome."

As he stood in the small courtyard garden, Caratacus ran his hand over his face. It was a strange feeling. He had not been clean-shaven since his youth. Eurgain had implored him to do so. As they were now captives in all but name, and did not wish to be made a spectacle of, it would be best if they made themselves look like Romans. While he had shaved, Caratacus elected to wear a far more practical tunic rather than the more formal and cumbersome toga. On this particular day, he was expecting a visit from the emperor himself, who promised to pay his respects and see how the king and his family were assimilating to Roman life. Though they had recently been mortal enemies, Emperor Claudius treated Caratacus almost as if he were a personal friend. It was still early in the day, and the visitor who beat on the large double doors of the outer courtyard was the last person he ever expected or wanted to see.

Caratacus' face hardened as the doors opened and his brother strolled into the garden. His face was freshly shaved, his hair cropped short, and he wore a formal Roman toga. It even bore the narrow purple stripe Caratacus learned denoted a member of the imperial lesser-nobility. There was something about Amminus' demeanour, however. A sense of sorrow and regret. His fist clenching his tunic, Caratacus fought to supress his utter hatred for his brother, whose throat he wished to tear out with his bare hands. So great was his fury that he found himself unable to speak.

"Brother," Amminus said, nodding almost to the point of a bow. "It gladdens me to see that you live, and are being treated well."

Eurgain came into the garden from the east wing, her eyes widening at the sight of her brother-in-law. Her teeth clenched, face red with anger, as she made ready to scream a torrent of abuse at him. Caratacus raised his hand, silencing her before she could unleash.

"What is it you want?" he asked, fighting his rage, his voice quiet and hoarse. "Have you come to gloat over your fallen kinsman? That we are prisoners of Rome is not enough for you?" Finally he could contain his emotions no longer. *"Aeron damn you, Amminus!"* His eyes were wet with tears of hatred. *"Why?"*

For all his previous senses of confidence and triumph, after witnessing his brother's defeat at Caer Caradoc, Amminus now struggled to find the words he needed.

"I did what I had to," he finally said, tears streaming down his cheeks. Unlike his brother, he wept from pent up anguish brought on by the horrific guilt of having betrayed his own family. "The Romans have rewarded me greatly, yet each toast in my honour tastes like a bitter poison. Every gift and honour they bestow upon me scorches my soul like burning coals. My quarrel was with our father, and when he died I longed for nothing more than to return home, yet our brother would not allow it."

"Togodumnus never forgave you," Caratacus conceded.

"And yet I still loved him. You may think I'm a liar, but I wept for him when he was slain."

"He was killed by those who murdered and enslaved your own people; the very people you betrayed!"

"I have no people!" Amminus shouted in despair. "When Father had me exiled, I was no longer a Catuvellauni. I had no home, no tribe, and no family! What was I to do?"

Caratacus hardened his heart, refusing to allow his brother's words to move him. "Well, you've had your revenge. Am I supposed to pity you now?"

"Not pity," Amminus said, slowly shaking his head. He composed himself and took a deep breath, struggling with his next words. "What I have come to ask is much more difficult than simple pity. I am here to ask your forgiveness."

Caratacus was dumbfounded by this. Amminus, who had stood triumphant with the Romans at Caer Caradoc, who had helped destroy the alliance against the invaders, was now asking—almost begging—for his forgiveness. He turned away for a few moments, composing his thoughts. Caratacus' fearsome rage was now replaced by a series of conflicting feelings. While much of him still hated his brother, another part of him did pity Amminus, strange and perverse as that seemed. He slowly began to accept why his emotions were so powerful. He knew he could never give his brother that which he most desired. He looked to Eurgain, whose own countenance showed she was equally conflicted. She gazed at her husband and gave a slow nod of consent.

"Amminus," he said calmly, his voice much calmer, still cracked with emotion. He stepped forward and placed both hands on his brother's shoulders, causing him to shudder. "As Rome is no longer my enemy neither are you. It will take some time, but I promise to

211

let go of the hate within my heart. You are a prince of Catuvellauni. But more importantly, you are my brother, and you have my love. But my forgiveness…" He shook his head sadly.

In that moment, both brothers understood.

"That is something I am unable to give you. And for that, I am sorry."

The two embraced and Amminus took his leave, giving a sad look of acknowledgment towards Eurgain before departing.

As he watched his brother walk through the gate, Caratacus knew he had seen him for the last time.

It was late afternoon when Emperor Claudius called upon Caratacus. For this, the former high king was thankful. It had taken much time to compose himself following his emotional final encounter with his brother. The emperor wore a simple toga this day, devoid of any formal trappings.

"Welcome, Caesar," Caratacus said with a bow. "You honour my house with your presence."

"Please, the honour is mine," Claudius said.

It surprised Caratacus that the emperor had ordered his guardsmen to stay within the garden and to leave the two alone. They walked together along the balcony that looked towards Capitoline Hill and the magnificent temples that dominated the city landscape.

"It is a splendid city," Caratacus said approvingly. "Far more magnificent than any I have ever seen."

"You had your own forms of wealth," Claudius replied. "I have seen your old kingdom, and it is beautiful in its own right."

"And I am sorry I will never see it again. But from what I have seen, Rome is truly blessed by the divines." He paused and clutched the stone rail, unsure how he should word his next question. "Can I ask you something?"

"You are my guest, and a friend of Caesar," Claudius reassured him. "You can ask me anything."

Caratacus took a deep breath. "Why did you come to Britannia? What was there in our land that Caesar so desired? How can you, who lords over the world with an empire of splendour worthy of the gods, covet our poor tents?"

Historical Afterward

Caratacus and his family remained in Rome, where they lived out their days as guests of the Caesars. His date of death is unrecorded, though as he is not mentioned at all during the reign of Vespasian, one can assume he died prior to 69 A.D. Whatever his status or eventual fate, Caratacus and his family were certainly not treated as slaves. The villa given to them by Emperor Claudius became known as the *Palatium Britannicum*. The 4th century Church of Santa Pudenziana is thought to be built upon the same site. Caratacus' daughter would go on to marry a Roman senator named Rufus, adopting the name Claudia Rufina and becoming a Roman citizen herself.

A 17th century image of Caratacus

Amminus returned to Britannia, where he was treated as a prince of the peoples under Roman dominion and also became a Roman citizen. He was likely made a member of the equites or senatorial class; a not uncommon status given to wealthy allied nobility who became citizens. He married a Roman woman of noble origins, further strengthening alliances between the empire and indigenous nobles. Amminus' son, Sallustius Lucullus, would serve as Governor of Britannia from 84 to 89 A.D. An inscription was found in Chichester, England, not far from the Roman Palace at Fishbourne, which is dedicated to *'Lucullus, son of Amminus'.* Through his Roman nephew, the bloodline of Caratacus lorded over more of Britannia than even the greatest Catuvellauni kings.

Ostorius Scapula was awarded *Triumphal Ornaments* for his defeat of Caratacus, even though resistance to Roman rule continued in Wales. His health continued to decline, and he died just two years after his decisive victory at Caer Caradoc. His final resting place is thought to be in the Vale of Glamorgan, the southernmost county in Wales. A statue in his honour was erected on the terrace of the Roman Baths located in Bath, England, in the 19th century.

Statue of Ostorius Scapula
The Roman Baths, Bath, England

The isle of Britannia proved to be a very difficult province for the Romans to subdue. Scapula's immediate successors, Didius Gallus (52 to 57 A.D.), Quintus Veranius (57 A.D. died soon after taking office) and Suetonius Paulinus (57 to 61 A.D.) fought a series of wars, both against rebellious provincials, as well as the still-unconquered regions of Wales. While arable land was the true measure of any province's wealth, the plethora of valuable metals made Wales one of the foremost regions for mining within the Roman Empire. Vast complexes were built to harvest copper, tin, lead, silver, zinc, and iron. Though perhaps greatest of all, in terms of wealth-producing, were the gold mines at Dolaucothi. Scholars and archaeologists had attempted, unsuccessfully, to ascertain the volume of gold extracted. Given that Dolaucothi was still in use through Victorian times, the amount of gold mined by the Romans is thought to be considerable. Today, one can still tour the old Roman mining tunnels, and see first-hand the marks left by tens-of-thousands of pickaxes over the near-four centuries of Roman rule.

The Deceangli continued for some time to resist the rule of Rome, namely due to the strong influence of the local druids. They made their stronghold on the Isle of Anglesey, where they were destroyed by the armies of Suetonius Paulinus in 61 A.D., just prior to the Iceni rebellion under Queen Boudicca. After which, the Deceangli disappeared from historical record.

Due to the horrific losses suffered at Caer Caradoc, the **Ordovices** were subdued and remained docile for twenty years. In the 70s A.D., they rose in rebellion, nearly wiping out a regiment of Roman cavalry that was garrisoned in their territory. The Roman governor at the time, Julius Agricola, unleashed a merciless campaign of annihilation against the Ordovices. According to Tacitus, Agricola succeeded in exterminating the entire tribe. While it is highly unlikely that the entire population was wiped out, they disappeared from all historical records. Survivors were likely either enslaved or scattered and assimilated into other tribes.

The peace made between Rome and the **Demetae** would, surprisingly, endure. Their territory was one of the few regions where imperial troops were never stationed. And yet their volatile neighbours, the Silures, made no concerted attempt to conquer their lands. Around 75 A.D. they were elevated to a Roman *civitas*, or 'Romanized state'. Their capital was founded at Moridunum, in what is now Carmathen, just north of the River Towy. Of all the ancient tribal kingdoms in Wales, the Demetae were the only ones allowed to maintain both their name, as well as at least some semblance of their indigenous culture. Villas that have been excavated have shown most settlements to be decidedly pre-Roman, albeit with some upgrades in masonry and plumbing that came after the conquest. This suggests that, unlike eastern Britannia, the Demetae maintained a measure of independence and were never fully integrated into Roman culture.

The ever-warlike **Silures** proved to be among the hardest peoples for the Romans to subdue. Subsequent Roman governors tried both diplomacy and force to bring them to heel. Tacitus praises the Silures for their 'natural ferocity', further stating that 'neither severity nor clemency converted them'. Agricola's predecessor, Sextus Julius Frontinus, fought a long, bitter campaign against the Silures from 75 to 78 A.D. During this time, he established the permanent legionary fortress for Legio II, Augusta, at a place called Isca, in what is now Caerleon in Wales. Other Roman forts were established near Chepstow and Caerwent. It was only with such an overwhelming and permanent presence of imperial troops within their lands that the Silures were finally tamed. The town of Venta Silurum, now known as Caerwent, was established as the civilian administrative capital of the newly-conquered tribe.

Though Ostorius Scapula's decisive victory shattered Caratacus' alliance, it is still a tribute to the tenacity of the resistance fighters that Wales was not fully conquered and assimilated into the Roman Empire until twenty-seven years after Caer Caradoc.

The Roman amphitheatre in Caerleon, established around 78 A.D. Located just outside the fortress, it served as both an entertainment venue as well as a drill field for legionaries.

Made in the USA
San Bernardino, CA
06 September 2016